D0053261

THE PLEASURE OF HIS COMPANY

Campaign picture commissioned by the candidate in spring, 1946. Inscription: "For Red Who cracked the joke which produced the smile from his old friend. The Candidate — April 1946."

PAUL B. FAY, JR.

THE

PLEASURE OF

HIS

COMPANY

HARPER & ROW, PUBLISHERS
NEW YORK, EVANSTON, AND LONDON

To my Children
Kathy, Paul and Sally,
but most
to my wife, Anita,
the Bride

ILLUSTRATIONS

Campaign picture, inscribed to author (frontispiece)

ACKNOWLEDGMENTS

Because of a comment made to me by the President of the United States in the late summer of 1963, I embarked on this labor of love, namely to retrace and attempt to record the many incidents and experiences—mostly happy, sometimes serious or sad, but always exciting—that I was privileged to share over a period of more than twenty years with John Kennedy.

To write this very unprofessional effort I needed and received help from many people in varying degrees. I now would like to acknowledge with sincere gratitude that invaluable help.

To the ladies who labored to transpose my often illegible scribblings into a typewritten manuscript: Dorothy Suares, Marian Mullen, Antoinette Whytoshek, Susan Long, Clara Vest Bell, Elvira Le Strange and Mary Robey.

To Enud S. McGiffert, who early in the going gave valuable critical advice.

To Joan Henricksen, who researched each line on each page with a thoroughness that would do justice to a space scientist before the final countdown.

To Sterling Lord for quiet sound counsel when a lesser man might have lost his objectivity.

To Rose Franco for her always pleasant composure and consistent refusal to allow emotions and personalities to interfere with the continuing process to publication.

To Evan Thomas, who earned equal to Ambassadorial status by his adroit handling of the different personalities and issues that seemed on occasion to stand between making his publication date or no publication at all.

To George "Barney" Ross, Mary Bailey Gimbel and Rowland Evans, who possibly unbeknownst to themselves gave sound counsel and direction when most needed.

To John Kenneth Galbraith, James A. Reed, Edmund W. Nash, Edward A. McDermott and John Carl Warnecke, who took the time to read the manuscript as it was approaching its final form and then to offer suggestions that to a great extent shaped its ultimate form.

To Senator Robert F. Kennedy for providing immeasurable help in identifying aspects which if left unchanged because of my literary immaturity and political ineptness could have caused me humiliation and reflected improperly on his brother, the late President. It should be explained that he read sections of a very early draft and cannot be held responsible for anything in the final script.

To Mrs. John F. Kennedy for her wisdom, patience and advice for which I have the most sincere and unqualified gratitude.

To Myrick Land without whose continuing help I question that this book could ever have been written, much less published.

You could see a laugh coming in his eyes before you could hear it from his lips.

—BENJAMIN BRADLEE

CHAPTER ONE

PRESIDENT JOHN F. KENNEDY was staying at the home he and Jacqueline rented on Squaw Island, near Hyannis Port, for the summer of 1963. My wife and I, along with our youngest daughter, Sally, were spending a weekend with them, and after the President and I played nine holes of golf at the Hyannis Port Club, he said, "Red, Lyndon is coming by around 7:15. Why don't you come down and join us?"

"It's great with me," I said. "How about the Bride?"

"Fine," he said.

Because I knew the President liked to dress informally when he was on the Cape, I decided to wear a Navy blue blazer

1

with a pair of raspberry-colored slacks he had bought for me the previous Easter at Palm Beach, Florida.

During that same Florida shopping trip, he had selected some lemon-colored slacks for himself, and when I came downstairs with my wife Anita I found that he was wearing those slacks, a pale blue sport shirt and a Navy blue blazer.

The Vice President, who was about to leave on an official trip, came in a few minutes later, followed by George Reedy.

"Lyndon, do you know Anita and Red Fay?" the President asked.

With his very gracious Southern manner, the Vice President responded, "Why, yes, I certainly know Anita and Red," and shook our hands. We were then introduced to George Reedy, whom I had not met before.

When we were all seated, I was strongly conscious of the contrasts in the room. Reedy was sniffing and snorting, and his hair seemed to be shooting off in all directions. The apparent uneasiness and unsureness of the Vice President surprised me more. He was dressed for his trip in a double-breasted blue suit that seemed unusually somber in contrast to the blazer and slacks worn by the trimly dressed President, and he sat forward uncomfortably on the edge of his seat.

As I watched the Vice President, I remembered a brief exchange I had had with him after a small reception he and I both attended in honor of astronaut John Glenn several months earlier. Before going on to dinner, about twenty guests met in the offices of Secretary of the Navy Fred Korth for drinks. The Vice President and I were the last two to leave the Secretary's office.

"You know, Red," he said to me that evening, "you're

really lucky. You've got a job where you've got responsibility. When you give an order, it's carried out. You're important to the Navy as well as the Defense Department. You're doing something for your country. What have I got? Nobody cares whether I come or I don't come. I don't even know why I'm here."

As Under Secretary of the Navy, a man near the bottom of the Washington protocol ladder, I found myself saying, "But, Mr. Vice President, you're darned important. You're doing a fantastic job."

"You're nice to say that, but . . ." he said.

As we walked down the hall to the dining room, I thought to myself, "Could there be a more ludicrous scene than this? Here I am, Red Fay, trying to bolster the spirits of the Vice President of the United States, hoping to keep him happy in his job."

That evening at Squaw Island, Johnson went over his itinerary with the President. His trip had been carefully planned in cooperation with the State Department, and would cover the Scandinavian countries. But suddenly Johnson said:

"I think it would be a good idea to expand my itinerary to include a visit to Poland. It would be a dramatic sign of our desire to be friendly with the countries behind the Iron Curtain, particularly those that have shown a desire for freedom."

I could see that Jack was taken by surprise. His reaction was to sit quietly, listening motionlessly and intensely. When the Vice President finished, the President asked simply, after a moment's pause, "Has this been cleared by the State Department?"

"No," the Vice President said, "I didn't want to start any planning until I got your reaction."

After another pause, the President said, "I don't think such a trip is a good idea at this time. Maybe some time later."

Then, to ease a rather strained moment, the President asked in a friendly, relaxed way: "What do you plan to talk about on your trip? If you have a prepared speech, I'd like to see it."

The Vice President turned to Reedy.

"George, let me have a copy of my speech."

This request set Reedy into motion on a somewhat frantic search through a briefcase. When this failed to produce the document, he mumbled something about "out in the car," and hurried out of the room, returning shortly with the speech.

The President started to read it. Almost immediately he paused and asked for a pencil. Receiving it, he started reading again. Everyone else remained silent. He turned the pages so rapidly, pausing now and then to stop and cross out a paragraph or a line, that it seemed hard to believe that he had read even the first quarter of each page. When he finished, he turned to Lyndon.

"I think it is very good," he said. "I have crossed out a few short sections which won't hurt the speech but which are better unsaid."

A few minutes later, the meeting broke up with the President wishing the Vice President the best of luck on his trip.

When the Vice President and George had left, I asked the President, "What was the pitch about wanting to go to Poland?"

"The poor guy's got the lousiest job in government, and just wants to make a significant contribution," the President

4

replied sympathetically. "Unfortunately the timing isn't right. Otherwise I'd love to see him go and have a little fun."

"You have no idea of how different your meeting was from what I thought it was going to be," I said.

The President seemed mildly intrigued.

"What do you mean?" he asked.

"Lyndon seemed so ill at ease, almost unsure of himself with you. It was so surprising because you've always gone so far in recognizing his importance to your administration."

This observation seemed to interest him. After a moment, he said to me, "Redhead, you've had an exposure of the Presidency that few people have had. You've got an obligation to write about it."

Soon after, I began making notes for this book. Being neither a professional writer nor an historian, I had no intention of attempting to compete with the distinguished historians and literary figures who were already preparing their own records of the Kennedy years. Instead, I wanted to try to reconstruct the story of the twenty-one years from my first meeting with John Kennedy in 1942, focusing on the episodes that reveal some aspects of the personality of the thirty-fifth President of the United States that might be overlooked or obscured in the works which concentrate on great public questions and international crises.

This, then, is the journal of a friendship. I would like to begin by recalling a December afternoon in 1959 when almost casually a remarkable family determined the date for its most brilliant member to make the official announcement of his candidacy for the Presidency.

CHAPTER TWO

NE AFTERNOON IN December, 1959, Joseph Kennedy, Jack and Jacqueline, Bobby and Ethel, my wife and I sat on the patio of Mr. Kennedy's home in Palm Beach. We were enjoying a few quiet moments before lunch, after a morning of swimming, tennis and touch football.

Suddenly the relaxed air was broken by Bobby demanding, "All right, Jack, what has been done about the campaign? What planning has been done?"

Jack did not answer immediately, and Bobby continued with increasing intensity: "Jack, how do you expect to run a successful campaign if you don't get started? A day lost now can't be picked up on the other end. It's ridiculous that more work hasn't been done already."

Jack leaned over toward me and began mimicking Bobby's voice: "How would you like looking forward to that voice blasting into your ear for the next six months?"

Then he turned to Bobby without a pause and said, "All right, Bobby, we've been able to do a few things in your absence, but we're very appreciative of your support and intend to call on it extensively."

For half an hour, the total attention of everyone there in the patio was concentrated on the forthcoming campaign. Jack reviewed precisely what had been done and then outlined the necessary steps for the future. The two brothers discussed key political figures who could—or could not— be counted on to lend their support. For some reason the name of Mike DiSalle, the Governor of Ohio, sticks in my mind as someone they thought could be relied on at that early date.

The meeting of the minds on this and so many other occasions was an illustration of the mutual respect, admiration and confidence that these two talented brothers felt toward each other. Although they were different in personality— Bob the more serious and intense, Jack the complete man—the older brother's open admiration for his younger brother's clear, sound, balanced judgment was never exceeded by his feeling toward anyone else who was part of his administration as long as he lived. That Bob Kennedy was held just as high in the President's affection made it doubly pleasant.

That day in Palm Beach had started like almost all other

Kennedy days, with the accent on total participation in a brisk swim in the ocean before breakfast.

At breakfast, practically every newspaper from New England, New York and Washington was scattered around the table, and the contents of the papers were consumed with greater hunger than the food.

I had learned long before that it was always advisable to read the national and international news and to give special attention to the latest pronouncements of the leading columnists if you wished to be prepared for the moment when the Senator from Massachusetts arrived on the scene.

It was not unusual to have Jack walk in, draped only in skivvy shorts and a pajama top, and comment with feeling: "Did you read what that S.O.B. ——— ——— said about . . . ?" or "Did you see how Reston cut up that poor ———?"

After breakfast that morning, we had the inevitable game of touch football. Jack masterminded the attack on our side. Unless I played as if I were the prize rookie of the National Football League, I knew the kind of reception I would get from him back in each huddle: "My God, can't you cut any faster than that? I laid that pass out in front of you like Johnny Unitas." Or: "Do you know that I haven't seen daylight between you and Bobby yet? Are you trying to make him look good?" Only on occasion would he admit that he might have contributed to our less-than-brilliant team showing. "The Old Master might have released the ball just a split second too soon," he'd confess, while rallying us for the next play.

After the game, we all went for a swim in the Grecian pool just off the south patio. At one end was a ten-foot-square box, open to the sky, which contained some cushioned benches and several wicker chairs for sunbathing. It also served as Joseph Kennedy's open-air office. He would settle there after his morning horseback ride and breakfast, with a telephone at his elbow and his notebook in his lap. Even when he was wearing swimming shorts and was covered with suntan lotion, with perspiration running down his cheeks, chin and chest, Joe Kennedy was still an impressive figure. Although you could not hear what he was saying, you could feel the power in that voice as he directed one of the great American business empires from his post there beside the pool.

That night, just before dinner, Joseph Kennedy said something that has always puzzled me.

Since I was dressed before the others, I went into the small bar-TV room just off the dining room, to make some daiquiris. Joseph Kennedy came in a few minutes later. We were alone.

Almost as if he were thinking out loud he said, "Jack is going to have a rough time. He's young and has to fight the issue of being a Catholic. The economy is too good. There doesn't seem to be a real threat of war. I hate to see him and Bobby working so hard if the timing is all wrong."

He had hardly finished talking when Jack and Jacqueline entered the room. Jack made some remark about the campaign, and Mr. Kennedy stated emphatically, "Jack, I'm willing to bet one million dollars today with the gamblers in Las Vegas that you'll win the nomination and election."

I was astonished. He didn't even glance at me to acknowledge our earlier conversation, yet he had made a 180-degree change of position in less than sixty seconds.

If I had reflected a few moments, I wouldn't have been so perplexed. I believe Mr. Kennedy, in spite of his own per-

9

sonal reservations, acknowledged Jack's and Bob's superior judgment about political timing and felt they were closer to the current political scene. More important, they had his uncompromising support, since they had already made their decision to embark on a particular political venture.

Several nights later, we had a discussion around the dinner table which I had never expected to hear at a Kennedy family gathering. The subject was family finances.

It is hard to remember how the conversation turned in that direction, but once it did Mr. Kennedy plunged in, fire blazing from his eyes.

"I don't know what is going to happen to this family when I die," Mr. Kennedy said. "There is no one in the entire family, except for Joan and Teddy, who is living within their means. No one appears to have the slightest concern for how much they spend." Warming up to his tirade, he went on: "I don't know what is going to happen to you all after I am gone."

Then he turned to one of the girls and said, "And you, young lady, you are the worst. There isn't the slightest indication that you have any idea what you spend your money on. Bills come in from all over the country for every conceivable item. It is utterly ridiculous to display such disregard for money."

At this point her husband stepped in. Directing his statement to Mr. Kennedy, he said, "I think you have made your point."

The chastened young lady burst into tears and ran out of the room, with her husband right after her. Realizing he had centered most of his wrath on only one of the girls, Mr.

Kennedy concluded in a slightly more subdued tone: "I just hope some of you girls try to live within your income, or your children are going to live an entirely different type of life."

A few minutes later, the couple came back. Everyone was still tense. Jack looked up and said, "Well, kid, don't worry. We've come to the conclusion that the only solution is to have Dad work harder."

Even Mr. Kennedy had to laugh.

Before my wife and I left for Christmas in San Francisco, plans were completed for Jack's announcement of his candidacy for the Democratic nomination for President of the United States. As we all sat around the luncheon table in our shorts and sport shirts, on a beautiful windless sun-drenched Florida day, Eunice Kennedy Shriver, with her usual quick and uninhibited humor, was already forming a Cabinet. "Let's see now," she said. "Dad, you are Secretary of the Treasury. If Jack has trouble balancing the budget, he can ask you to make up the difference out of your own pocket. Bobby we'll make Attorney General so he can throw all the people Dad doesn't like into jail. That means we'll have to build more jails." So it went on—what at the time seemed like a most implausible list.

Finally Eunice got down to me. "Red Fay will be the Secretary of the Navy." Ethel Kennedy broke in, "If he runs the Navy the way he ran our boat on the cruise, we'll have a lot of carriers for landmarks."

The reference to Secretary of the Navy took me back many years to the time I was helping Jack in his first political campaign in Boston. At that time an old college classmate and

Zete fraternity brother, Curt Hayden, wrote me from San Francisco asking in jest, "Are you helping Jack Kennedy because you think he is going to make you Secretary of the Navy when he becomes the President of the United States?" I wrote back in the same vein: "No, Curt, it's not Secretary of the Navy but Under Secretary. . . ."

Fifteen years later my prophecy came true.

CHAPTER THREE

ARLY IN MARCH, 1960, Bob Kennedy telephoned me. "Jack wants you to come to Wisconsin for the last four or five days," he said. "Get Barney Ross to come too, because on Saturday night there is going to be a state-wide half-hour TV program, and Jack wants all the men who were on PT 109 with him to be on hand."

"Don't worry, Bob, I'll be there," I said. And then I asked him: "If I can get any more workers, do you want me to bring them along?"

"Whom do you have in mind?" Bob asked, with some apprehension in his voice.

"I'm quite sure I can get Dirty John Galvin. He was a great

pal of Jack's out in San Francisco at the end of the war, when they both spent some time at my family's place down at Woodside together." (In fairness to John, he got his nickname because of his obsession with cleanliness.)

The "great pal" bit might have been larding it up a little. Jack liked the Dirty One, but at that stage of the game he possibly might not have recognized him in passing.

Bob said okay, so on Thursday, March 31, I was on my way to Chicago to pick up Dirty John and Barney. John was ready to go, but Barney was another problem. He was working for an insurance broker and had great misgivings about pulling out on him for a day and a half, because of some report he had to have typed up for Monday morning. But in a few minutes we headed over to pick up Dirty John and Killer Kane (an old PT boat shipmate christened Robert who had flown in from Binghamton, New York) and then started for Milwaukee. Once we were there, we located the Kennedy headquarters on the main street, Wisconsin Avenue. There were all the usual features of a political headquarters: the professionals—in this case Pierre Salinger, Kenny O'Donnell and Larry O'Brien—quietly at work in the center of all the confusion and near chaos, girls typing like mad, shy enthusiasts wanting to climb on the bandwagon but hesitating because they weren't sure where the step was, and, of course, the panhandler who just needed a couple of bucks and was ready in return to get four guys to switch to John Kennedy.

"Redhead, I have to get out this report before I do anything," Barney said as soon as we arrived. "I'll see if I can borrow a typewriter."

I made a quick estimate of the typing job.

14

"Barney, you came up here to campaign, not to pore over some insurance report. We'll find some eager, attractive typist who will be overcome by your basic charm and get this whole job done in less than an hour."

We immediately started to "case" the premises for a likely victim. The best-looking young lady in the headquarters had stopped for a moment to comb her hair. This momentary lapse made her a marked target. She turned out to be as nice as she was lovely, and her name was Pam Turnure. In her quiet voice she responded, "Sure, what do I have to do?"

We left Barney and Pam to complete a series of insurance accident reports. Killer, Dirty and I filled our pockets with campaign buttons and pamphlets, and walked out onto the main street.

We approached everyone we could with such pleas as: "If you aren't already committed, would you cast your vote for John Kennedy?" or "Will you help elect John Kennedy President of the United States?" I always liked the second approach.

We hadn't been out on Wisconsin Avenue for more than an hour on that gray April afternoon before the candidate himself wheeled up before the headquarters in a Wisconsin-manufactured Rambler station wagon, with the car's loudspeaker blaring: "Vote for John Kennedy for your next President."

From where we were working the sidewalk we could see Jack go into the headquarters. All the workers came forward just to see the candidate or to hear a few words from him. "You're doing a great job," Jack would say, or "Keep up the good work," or "Your contribution really counts." His exit was almost as fast as his entrance. Minutes later, Jack was

15

walking along the sidewalk greeting all the passers-by, while the station wagon followed slowly along, playing a song extolling the candidate.

He spotted Dirty, Killer and me.

"Would you fellows please spread out a little?" he asked. "I don't think this city is ready for such a high concentration of it in one location."

Turning to me, he said, "Redhead, jump in here with me. I haven't had any lunch. A restaurant down here a couple of blocks has the best ham and cheese sandwiches you'll ever eat." Piling into the back seat, which was bulging with sound equipment, pamphlets, buttons and all the paraphernalia of a political campaign, we headed toward the restaurant.

Although it was about four in the afternoon and very few people were in the restaurant, those who were there immediately recognized the handsome, smiling candidate. The owner ushered us over to a table near the window. We both ordered soup, ham and cheese sandwiches and cold German beer. I'd been carrying a five-dollar bill that an old classmate of mine at Stanford, Jake Thompson, had given me to give to the Senator. I pulled it out of my wallet and gave it to Jack.

"Jack," I said, "Jake Thompson asked me to give you his five for the campaign. He realizes it isn't much, but it is better than a poke in the eye with a sharp stick."

Taking the bill, Jack replied, "Tell old Jake—" whom Jack had never met—"we are taking it all, large and small."

Then we started to talk about the forthcoming TV program the next evening. "So that we all see this program in the same context," he said, "this is not a half-hour to give the State of Wisconsin an opportunity to get to know and love Ross and Fay. Leave 'Hooray for Hollywood' and 'McNamara's Band'

16

for the privileged few. We are going to considerable expense to project the candidate. There should be a short—I repeat, short —introduction by each of you, tying us all together in the great war effort, and then the candidate takes over. Whatever you do, don't give Bill Johnston more than just a chance to mention his name. Given an open field, Johnston would blow the whole war record of the candidate." (Bill was one of the motor mechanics on PT 109 when it was sunk.)

"How do we play Dirty John?" I asked. "Killer, Barney and myself are easy, but Dirty only has a little flight training to his credit incorporating a few ground loops."

Jack thought for a second. Then he said, "Just be very vague. Mention Navy, John and the war. Nobody's going to be too concerned about details."

Jack flagged down our waiter. When the check came, he laid down Jake Thompson's five-dollar bill to cover the $3.85.

"Tell old Jake when you see him that he bought a lunch for the candidate and his friend which at that moment kept the campaign going."

On the walk back to the headquarters, Jack stopped every few steps to greet whoever passed.

"My name is John Kennedy," he would say. "I would appreciate your vote in the primary."

He was at his best when some loud-mouth tried to embarrass him. One in his early twenties said, "Kennedy, I hear that your dad has only offered two dollars a vote. With all your dough can't you do better than that?"

Slightly irritated, Jack shot back, "You know that statement is false. It's sad that the only thing you have to offer is your vote, and you're willing to sell that."

That evening, Jack and Jacqueline were scheduled for an 8

17

P.M. rally at a Polish hall about forty-five minutes outside of Milwaukee. Barney, Killer, Dirty and I were informed that the candidate wanted us out there to take a bow. We got a ride out with one of the volunteers, arriving about quarter of eight.

The hall, which could comfortably accommodate about fifteen hundred, was jam-packed with about three thousand people. Although it was pleasantly cool outside, the overcrowding and lack of air conditioning forced the temperature up into the nineties. At about 8:10 all the people who were to appear on the program except Jack and Jacqueline filed up on the stage.

Congressman Clem Zablocki announced: "Senator and Mrs. Kennedy will be a little late. Let's sing a few songs to give them a real Polish-American greeting when they arrive."

Clem was able to keep them singing for about twenty minutes, but the heat and the waiting soon took their toll. The crowd, having spent more than an hour waiting to get into the hall, now stood and sat in almost sullen silence.

Finally, about ten minutes before nine, the Senator and Jacqueline arrived to polite, subdued applause. Clem Zablocki said, "There was a mix-up in the schedule. The Senator had been told we were about five minutes from his headquarters instead of forty-five minutes." But the excuse fell on deaf ears. Clem then introduced Jacqueline. In her soft voice, she said simply, "We're terribly sorry to have kept you waiting so long when you'd been so nice to come. With so much to do in a campaign, it's a wonder that more mistakes aren't made which inconvenience people who are so kind and thoughtful as to encourage the candidate."

18

You could feel the tensions in the room running away, like a receding wave.

"I have great respect and affection for the Polish people; besides, my sister is married to a Pole," Jacqueline continued. Then in perfect Polish she stated, "Poland will live forever," and sat down.

The crowd burst into cheering and unashamed weeping.

Jack turned back to me and said, "How would you like to try and follow that?"

Thanks to a very lovely young lady the Polish vote in and around Milwaukee was saved for the Senator from Massachusetts.

Early the next evening, while Jack was continuing his campaigning, Barney, Dirty, Killer and I, with the aid of several cold draft beers, smoothed out a TV text in which we introduced each other, covered our war records and then told something about our present activities and types of business. We were all satisfied that we would present the image of four former heroes who had established themselves as executives in the fields of used cars, insurance and heavy construction. Somewhere in between, a rather indefinite image of the candidate filtered through.

About ten minutes before camera time, the candidate arrived. He immediately gathered us all in an anteroom just off the main hall and asked for a run-through on the script we had prepared for the TV show. Rather self-consciously we unfolded the sequence that we had enthusiastically hammered out over the beers, growing more delighted with the production with each beer.

Viewing the whole performance with a certain humor which was fortified by the realization that this little TV series was due to close before it ever opened, Jack said, "I realize the obvious material benefits to the entire cast if we screen such a performance, but tonight is not 'Help an old shipmate night.' We are trying to elect a candidate. This is the way we will put on the performance."

Within a few minutes, he scripted a half-hour program. He tossed overboard "old shipmates" commercials and opened instead with a string of introductions that reviewed our war experiences briefly and effectively. The remaining three-quarters of the time was spent on the candidate—which, we had to agree, was the purpose of the drill.

Clear and precise as the instructions were, the actual performance was a little shy of our expectations.

We entered the hall from the rear, and started up the main aisle to the stage. Women began screaming, and men were yelling, "We're for you, Jack."

I had been associated with President Eisenhower at a relative distance in the 1952 and 1956 campaigns, but this reception had a quality of mass dedication I had never experienced before. It reminded me of the excitement during Jack's first political campaign in 1946. After a while the excited audience finally settled down to hear the program. I was introduced as "a wartime buddy in PT boats who came all the way from San Francisco to help his old shipmate Jack Kennedy."

As I remember my historic lines, they went something like this:

"I've known Jack Kennedy since 1942 when we served together in PT boats. Even in those dark days during the fighting

20

in the South Pacific, he had a sense of dedication to his country that was a guiding light for all of us. I was proud to serve with him in PT's and I hope to serve as an American with John Kennedy as my President."

With this reference to Jack, the crowd began whistling and screaming again. I introduced Killer Kane, and then Barney Ross.

Barney said, "Before introducing the candidate, I'd like you to know one more of Jack's shipmates, John Galvin from Chicago. John wasn't in PT's but he was there in his airplane—" at this point, Barney put his hand over his head, making circling motions—"flying around looking out for us."

John stepped up to the microphone. "There wasn't one of us, whether on the water or in the air, that wouldn't have followed Jack wherever he led us," he said. "Thank you."

This was one of the shortest speeches John had ever given, for a good reason. John, who will never be accused of being a shy, retiring type, had never been in the South Pacific and had not known Jack until after the war.

Then Barney introduced Bill Johnston. Bill had hardly gotten the first two words out of his mouth before Barney was saying, "Thanks very much, Bill," ending his presentation.

Then Barney introduced Jack. The hall went wild.

While we were waiting for the audience to end the tremendous ovation, Jack stepped back from the microphone. He said quietly to us, "At any future gathering of this collection of war heroes, let's make sure we take Dirty John out of the sky and put him on one of the boats. We can't afford to take the risk of possibly belittling the great war record of the candidate by bringing in another dimension."

Jack made his last major speech of that campaign, except for a talk at the University of Wisconsin in Milwaukee on Monday. With the election set for Tuesday, all that we could do was wait till the voters recorded their choice.

After the TV program we went to dinner at the restaurant where Jack and I had eaten the afternoon before. Everyone who was on the TV program was at the dinner, along with Jacqueline, Ethel, Dorothy Tubridy and Eunice Kennedy Shriver.

I remember the dinner particularly because of the thoughtfulness of Jacqueline. Everyone obviously hoped to sit near the Senator. Jacqueline came up to me and in her soft, hushed voice said, "Red, Jack will probably ask you or one of his other close friends to sit next to him. See if you can't arrange it so Bill Johnston and his wife sit near him because they came all the way from Boston and never get a chance to see him."

This is the way the seating was arranged. One former PT motor mechanic, now a truck driver from Boston and no less impressive an individual for the change, and his wife had the seats of honor next to the future President of the United States and the future First Lady. Bill Johnston will always be able to tell his children and his grandchildren that to the thirty-fifth President of the United States he was not only a shipmate but more—a friend.

22

CHAPTER FOUR

ITH AN INCREASING number of primary victories behind him, Jack scheduled a brief visit to the Bay area in April to solidify his position with some of the local political chieftains in San Francisco and to return to Stanford University for a speech. He had called me several days earlier, asking if I wanted to accompany him on the Stanford visit.

Quentin "Cootie" Thompson, a great Stanford baseball star, classmate, fraternity brother and pal of mine, and I drove down to the Hilton at the San Francisco Airport to meet him. When we arrived, there was no doubt that the candidate was somewhere about. We could feel the excitement that always prevailed wherever he moved. Walking down the main hall of the hotel with Coot, I spotted Pierre Salinger.

"Redhead, how are you?" Pierre said. "The Senator is having a meeting with some of the political figures from San Francisco. Go right in. He'd love to see you."

I walked into the room where Jack was holding forth. Either my entrance was something of a shock to all present or else they were observing a moment of silence for some departed friend. When I walked over to say hello to Jack, I had a strong feeling that I was an outsider who had just entered a secret meeting at the most secret moment.

I had no sooner gotten out my self-conscious greeting—"Jack, great to see you. How are things going?"—than the Senator began gently but firmly turning me around and heading me back toward the door.

"Red, would you go out in the hall and help Pierre guard the door so that we can run this gathering without any interruptions?" he asked. "I'll see you later."

Once outside, still slightly shaken by the whole episode, I asked Pierre, "God, why did you ever let me in there? I could feel the temperature drop as if I were entering a cold-storage refrigerator."

Pierre somewhat sheepishly replied, "I thought you were part of the big picture here in San Francisco."

"As a registered Republican," I said, "I have the impression that I'm viewed very much like an informer scouting the enemy's strategic meetings. I'm just tolerated because of the Senator."

After a few minutes, the political powwow broke up and the candidate came out. Jack spotted Cootie and me. He started to head our way, but was intercepted by Pierre and several others who had arranged for a limousine caravan down to Stanford. Standing in one of his characteristic poses, with the right hand in his side coat pocket, he listened patiently as Pierre told him of the planned motorcade.

"This is the only chance I'll have to visit with two of Stanford's legendary figures so I'll drive down with **Red and** Cootie," Jack said, pleasantly but firmly. Turning to us, he continued, "I'm surmising that you have a car."

Coot could hardly blurt out fast enough, "Senator, we have the wheels."

"Have the other cars follow us down, as Coot and Red know exactly where we have to go," Jack said to Pierre.

A very frustrated Pierre lined up the limousines, and all headed down the Bayshore highway behind Cootie's new Ford sedan.

Jack talked of the progress of the campaign and expressed unmistakable optimism over his chances of getting the nomination. He did feel a certain anxiety about California, and speculated over whether Pat Brown was going to vacillate on his agreement of support.

"I told Pat I had no desire to come into California and get in a fight with him in the primary," Jack said. "It would split the party, and could lead to the Republicans regaining control. Besides, we took a poll in California which indicated I would beat Pat easily. I showed him the poll and he agreed to give me his support. As of now, I have yet to see or hear that he has come out publicly pledging me that support."

Pat Brown's role in these preconvention days has been widely misrepresented and misunderstood. There might be room to

25

criticize him for his timing (which is a matter of judgment), but there is no ground for accusing him of backing down on his word.

Pat agreed to come out for Jack and hoped to bring the whole California delegation to the convention with him. He also agreed not to enter the race for Vice President. It was accepted by both men that if two Catholics ran for the two top positions on the ticket, this most likely would ruin the chances of both. The question of when Pat would publicly throw his support to Jack was left up to Pat.

When Pat had not moved by April, Joe Kennedy and Hy Raskin met with the Governor in the Governor's Mansion. Joe Kennedy in characteristic fashion bluntly asked, "Are you coming out for Jack or not?"

Pat replied, "Mr. Kennedy, I'll come out for Jack tonight if you ask me to, but it would be a mistake. Clair Engle would fight it. He has never been approached and feels he has been slighted. Without Clair the delegation could be split and Jack wouldn't get all the support he needs. Let me work on Clair."

"All right, we'll go along with that plan," Joe Kennedy said.

But Clair Engle refused to give his support until he felt the time was right. This delay became the basis of a sharp exchange between Bob Kennedy and Pat Brown on Thursday before the convention started. Bob wanted Pat to announce his support for Jack then, but Pat refused. He said he would announce on Sunday, because Clair Engle would not go along with the idea until then.

Jack started to reminisce about Stanford as we swung off the Bayshore highway that day, heading into Palo Alto and on to Stanford. We were not far from our destination when Jack,

26

who had been coughing a little, asked, "Is there some place around here that I can get some cough drops to relieve this damn cough?"

"Wherever we stop, we are going to have to do it in a hurry because we are due at the Memorial Hall at Stanford in about five minutes," I said.

Coot stopped the car, double parking tight against the car parked next to the curb. As he jumped out on the driver's side, he said, "I'll run into the drugstore and get some cough drops."

The words were hardly out of his mouth when we heard the sharp whine of metal scraping against metal. In his rush to get out of the car, Cootie had opened the door just wide enough to cleanly peel the chrome strip off one side of a passing car. Luckily that was the only damage, but the driver of the stripped car slammed on the brakes and came storming out.

He was a young, rather disheveled-looking man of about six feet two, who probably weighed around two hundred pounds. Before he could start his onslaught, Cootie said hopefully, "Now I realize that I tore the chrome strip off your car, but I am an insurance agent and can take care of all your expense. You will have no problems. Here is my card and license number. Unfortunately I'm in a great hurry and can't discuss it all now."

As Coot started to leave, the owner of the damaged car started shouting in a manner which could only end up in a fight: "Don't start giving me any of that fast talk, wise guy. You stripped the chrome off my car, and I don't want to have any brush-off from you or anybody else. Now I'm going to get a cop and get this thing settled right now."

The traffic from the caravan following us, together with the other cars trying to move down University Avenue, was backed up for blocks. Horns started blowing impatiently. I jumped out of the car and raced into the drugstore to get the cough drops. I was out in a few seconds with my mission accomplished, but Cootie was still engaged with the other driver, who had no intention of trying to settle the disagreement without an officer.

Cootie, seeing that he was making no headway, started trying to push the about ten feet of chrome strip into the young man's car, which, no matter how you angled it, could take only about six feet of it. In spite of the delay, Jack was thoroughly enjoying Cootie's dilemma. I leaned out the window and said, "Coot, we'll have to leave right away. The people waiting at Stanford aren't going to appreciate the Senator arbitrating a chrome-stripping incident on a street corner in Palo Alto while they cool their heels on the campus."

With this, Cootie thrust the long piece of chrome into the car as far as it would go, with about four feet of it still sticking out.

Resigned that further effort was not going to bring any greater success, he put his card on the hood of the damaged car and said, "If you want to recover the expense of this minor damage, contact my office, because I'm not staying here any longer. If you want to make any more of it right now, you've got your hands full."

Suddenly the fight left Coot's antagonist and we were again on our way.

"Coot," Jack said, "I couldn't have been more impressed by the conciliatory manner in which you brought that young fellow around to your way of thinking. I hope I'm as convincing explaining our delay to the student audience at Stanford as you were convincing that dechromed driver what a great deal he happened to drive into."

Jack's speech at Stanford was extremely successful. When he left the stage and tried to make his way to the car, the swirling crowd carried him in the general direction he was headed. Even President Wally Sterling of Stanford had to force himself along with the rest of the crowd to get close enough to express his appreciation.

Forced away from the Senator by the crowd, I spotted Professor Tom Barkley, an old friend of Jack's. Knowing Jack would love to at least say hello, I called, "Tom, come over—Jack would love to see you."

"I'd like to give him my congratulations and best wishes," Tom said, "but I don't want to impose."

"Tom, you couldn't impose."

Grabbing his arm, I forced our way into the path of the Senator. Spotting us together, Jack called, "Hello, Tom."

Tom congratulated him, and Jack had just time to ask, "Tom, is it true what Red Fay tells me, that you considered him one of your most promising students?"

Tom, a man of great integrity but also of generous nature, knowing full well that I had never made such a statement, took only a second to compromise his integrity to be generous: "Red had a very enviable record."

Jack was carried away, obviously trying to reply that he knew the fix was on.

Unable to get back to Cootie's car, Jack went back to the airport in one of the limousines. Coot and I followed.

The shadows of evening were running long across the taxiway as Jack waited for his plane to take him to one of the

29

valley towns to speak before the local Democratic organization. He seemed deep in thought, and no one disturbed his privacy. As the plane approached, he strolled over to Coot and myself. Reaching in his pocket, he pulled out the box of cough drops. Offering them to Coot, he said, "Coot, have a hundred-dollar cough drop."

He walked up the ladder to the plane and was off into the night.

CHAPTER FIVE

BOUT A WEEK before his birthday in May, Jack decided to bring Jacqueline to the Monterey Peninsula for four days of relaxation before the final preconvention rush. They asked my wife and me to come down and join them.

Although this was ostensibly a vacation, it included a certain amount of work. Hugh Sidey, of *Time,* was going to do a cover story on Jack for the magazine, and he joined us each morning on the porch outside the Senator's room to interview him for an hour or so.

Sidey looks, acts and dresses like a polite, intellectual, somewhat reserved Ivy League graduate. One of his great talents as a reporter is an ability to convince you that anyone that nice would never write a word that would trouble you or tarnish your image. The result, of course, is that you talk more freely to him than you would otherwise. He is sincere and he is honest, but he is also a reporter, so he ends up writing whatever he believes to be the truth, even if the individual interviewed might have liked to have his portrait drawn with softer lines. For each morning interview Jack placed our three chairs very carefully. If Sidey spoke to me, he could not see Jack at the same time. While most of the answers were to be given by Jack, if a question came up which he felt called for an answer by a moré objective viewer than himself, the question would be thrown to me. If Jack was satisfied with the way I was responding, he would swing his arm in a circle behind Sidey as an indication that I was doing well and should keep going. If he didn't like my response, an exaggerated look of pure horror would cross his face. This would generally shake me so that I would jumble and stammer my next answer thoroughly. This would invariably bring a perplexed look to Sidey's face. He obviously was wondering how someone could be seemingly articulate one moment and almost incoherent the next.

Sidey's questions were usually asked in chronological order, but he was trying at the same time to discover how various incidents and individuals, particularly Jack's parents, had shaped Jack's character and his career. When a particular question seemed too personal or led to an answer Jack thought might seem too self-satisfied, he would give a bantering answer. Hugh never joined in the joshing, but came back in a lower key, still pursuing his subject. He was particularly anxious to establish the influence of Joseph P. Kennedy on his children, and particularly on Jack. After several unrewarding sallies on this subject, Hugh directed the question to me.

"Red, how much influence do you feel that the Senator's father has had on his career? Do you feel that he is the motivating force behind the amazing drive and ambition of the entire family?"

Jack's look of real concern indicated that he wanted me to think very carefully before answering the question.

"Hugh," I replied, "I think that Mr. Kennedy has been the most vital force in the careers of the Kennedy men and women, particularly after they left grade school and entered high school and college."

Jack, grimacing, indicated by drawing his finger across his neck that I ought to cut off what I was saying. He was obviously irritated by my response. I felt that if I had continued along the lines on which I had started, Jack would have had no complaint. But since this was a subject on which he was highly sensitive, I felt it was best to bow out gracefully until I had an opportunity to discuss my proposed reply with him in private.

I begged off lamely. "Actually, Hugh, I don't feel I am the best person to evaluate the relationship between Jack or his brothers and sisters with their father and mother. I didn't get to know Mr. Kennedy and the rest of the family till most of them were full-grown."

As soon as Sidey had left, Jack jumped me.

"God, if I hadn't cut you off, Sidey could have headed his article, 'A vote for Jack is a vote for Father Joe.' That's just the material *Time* magazine would like to have—that I'm a

33

pawn in Dad's hands. That it's really not Jack Kennedy who is seeking the Presidency, but his father. That Joe Kennedy now has the vehicle to capture the only segment of power that has eluded him. That once in the White House it will be Dad directing the policy with Nice Jack agreeing, 'Right again, Dad.' "

As politically naïve as I rated myself, I still felt that I was right and Jack wrong. I was convinced that he was unrealistic and overly sensitive on the question of the public's conception of the contributions his father had made toward his success.

"Jack," I said "notwithstanding my political immaturity, can I please make my case in total?"

He gave me a look of tolerant acquiescence, so I went ahead.

"I had no intention to tell Hugh Sidey that you are a pawn in your father's hands, but I think it would be wrong not to state the obvious influence your dad has had on your life. You couldn't convince anyone that a father as dynamic and positive as yours didn't have an effect on your ideas and philosophy as you grew up. I think the real question is when did your ideas and philosophy no longer coincide with his. Your voting record and public expressions certainly clearly show wide differences in opinion and position. I'm sure Sidey knows all that, but is interested in what earlier influence your father had in motivating and stimulating you to enter political life which eventually ended up in your seeking the Presidency. With your permission I'd like to complete what Sidey must think is a hell of a stupid response and make the case as I just stated it."

Jack cut in. "Now let's have it once more so I can be sure that in the years to come I won't point back to this day in May as the time that Red Fay turned what appears to be a promising campaign into a colossal disaster."

"I want to tell Sidey that it is my impression—and it will be strictly an impression, because I didn't know you until after college and I'll make this point clear—from what I have been able to gather in conversations with you and your family, that during your years in school your dad was the key figure in encouraging a career in public service. That during your years in college, the Navy and immediately after that your dad was the one person whose opinion you cared most for—to make him proud and pleased with your accomplishments. But simply, as the years went on and you assumed greater and greater responsibility, you still enjoyed the approval of your father but it in no way compared to your own personal desire to do what was right."

I paused.

The Senator gave me a look of skepticism coupled with vague approval.

"All right," he said after a few seconds. "But don't forget this is supposed to be a helpful cover story on a promising candidate and not the kiss of death."

When we arrived at the Cypress Point Club, Hugh Sidey was there to see us tee off. I took him aside and completed my answer to his question.

When the cover story came out, Jack was generally pleased, but he did make a mild accusation that the magazine had attempted some character distortion. This was completely consistent with his chronic belief that writers felt an article could not be successful unless it contained some demeaning reflections. John Kennedy, like most public men, never built up an immunity to the press. As long as I knew Jack, he could read four or five different slants into an article that I either missed completely or didn't believe were intended.

With the interview behind him, Jack and I headed for the first tee.

"Now, with an opponent who is one of Stanford's all-time, all-round athletes who makes his living playing golf with his friends, I figure since I haven't been playing at all that you give me a stroke a hole and two on the five pars and we'll play for a dollar a hole," he said. Without waiting for my protest, he turned to his caddy, "Handsome Hank," as though we had reached complete agreement and asked, "If we only play ten or eleven holes, what holes should we play so as to end up playing the last holes along the ocean?" Hank laid out ten holes, ending with the fourteenth, fifteenth, sixteenth, seventeenth and eighteenth.

Finally I said, "Jack I couldn't possibly give you two strokes on any hole even if I played to scratch and I'm a six."

"All right," he said, "but I hope this is not indicative of California hospitality."

On the fifteenth hole we played from the back tee. The hole has breaking white ocean water to the rear and along the right side down about a twenty-foot drop. After a brief study of the shot, Jack took out a seven iron and hit a perfect shot dead on the pin all the way. The ball hit about ten feet in front and proceeded to bounce and roll up to the hole.

I was yelling, "Go in, go in." Jack was standing there with a look of horror on his face. The ball hit the pin and kicked to the side, about six inches from the cup. With a sigh of relief, he turned to me.

"You're yelling for that damn ball to go in the hole and I'm watching a promising political career coming to an end. If that ball had gone into that hole, in less than an hour the word

36

would be out to the nation that another golfer was trying to get in the White House."

Then he said, "If that group of people hadn't been watching from the road, I wonder what it would have cost me to have our two trusted caddies keep quiet till after the convention?"

After our golf game, we walked from the eighteenth green over to some tables set up on a patio facing west toward the ocean. Our wives joined us. We called for a waiter, to order a bowl of soup for Jack, a beer for myself and Cokes for the girls.

When the waiter, whose name was Sam, arrived, he politely admonished us, "Gentlemen, I'm very sorry I can't serve you out here unless you have on a coat and tie."

"Since there is no one here and our coats and ties are back at the Lodge, I'm sure the powers that be would be understanding and have no complaints if you served us just this once," I said in an almost pleading tone.

Seeing that my persuasive powers had had little or no effect on Sam, Jack added with a touch of jest: "After exposing himself to the demands of this great golf course, I'm sure the membership will excuse you the variance from the rules if you serve the tired old Senator." Then, shifting to a tone which assumed the waiter's acquiescence, he continued: "Bring Mrs. Fay and Mrs. Kennedy Coca-Colas, a Heineken's beer for Mr. Fay and a bowl of clear soup for me."

Sam nodded, and was back in a few minutes with our order. Soon Jack had him expounding on the wonders of the Cypress Point Club and the important people who played there, and talking about the complimentary letter from President Eisenhower now hanging in the front hall.

When we had completed our short respite under a warm

comfortable sun, I took off my golf shoes. Jack had taken his off earlier because he had developed a blister on each of his heels. (He had purchased the shoes in the golf shop just before playing.) We started to walk through the lounge of the club to get to our car.

Sam, who had come back to clean up the table, said, "Gentlemen, you're not allowed to go into the clubhouse without a coat and tie." The only people we had seen in the clubhouse area were young Sam Wolcott and a friend. They had already left.

"Jackie, you and Anita go through the lounge to the other side and if there is no one in sight, we'll come through," Jack said. "These damn feet of mine are killing me."

The girls walked through and then reported that the coast was clear. We followed then in our stocking feet. Within the week one of the leading local papers carried the story that the Senator from Massachusetts not only had refused to put on a coat and tie but had taken off his shoes on the patio for all to see.

The source for the newspaper story was not Sam the waiter, as we had at first suspected, but a prominent member. He also had said that Jacqueline Kennedy, who was still in her riding clothes from a morning ride, had walked the course in tight leotards, and that Senator Kennedy had sharply attacked the waiter when he was informed of the rules regarding dress. According to his story, the Senator told the waiter that he was a U.S. Senator and to hell with the rules—that Sam had better carry out his orders.

All of this garbage was sprung on me by several of my friends when I visited the Pacific Union Club in San Francisco.

My only comment was, "Your man is lying, and if he would like to get the truth from someone who was there I would be happy to fill him in."

What made this particularly strange was this same man's earlier graciousness to the Kennedys just after their wedding. In 1953, when Jack and Jackie visited the Cypress Point Club on their honeymoon, he had eagerly created an opportunity to have his picture taken with the Senator from Massachusetts. The only explanation I can propose is that in 1953 Jack Kennedy was not a candidate for a national office, but in 1960 he was—and politics does funny things to otherwise rational people.

Jack had felt the changed atmosphere around the club before that story appeared. He remarked to me during lunch on our third day there: "Redhead, the climate around here has perceptibly chilled. We're not the beloved figures of seven years back."

On the last day of the brief vacation, we played another ten holes of golf. After we had returned to the Del Monte Lodge, I opened the rear compartment of the car to get our street shoes and socks, and Jack spotted a football lying between the golf bags.

"Nobody will be going off the first tee this late," he said (referring to the first hole on the Pebble Beach Golf Course). "Why don't we go over onto the first fairway and throw the ball around for a while?"

"Great," I said.

After we had passed the ball back and forth several times, the Senator noticed a young fellow standing over by the golf shop watching us.

39

"Red," he suggested, "why don't you get that kid and somebody else so we can have a short game of touch?"

I soon had the young boy and the assistant golf pro lined up to play. First we explained the "Kennedy Rules." There was no blocking. You had to wait until the tailback received the ball from the center before you could cross the line of scrimmage and rush him. You could throw the ball anywhere anytime at any position on the field, either forward or backward.

As the two new players were considerably younger than we were, there was a question in my mind whether Jack and I should play as partners, particularly because the young caddy had told me that the assistant pro had been an all-league halfback several years back for Salinas Junior College. But that question was soon resolved when Jack said, "All right, we'll play you two." He pointed to the assistant pro and the caddy. "The first team to score three touchdowns wins. We'll kick off."

I asked him quietly, "Why did you limit it to the first team to score three touchdowns? Why don't we play till it starts to get dark? The girls are going to take that long to get ready for dinner."

"I'm going to cover the kid and I'm sure he'll be covering me," Jack said. "Based on my analysis of him, it will take him three touchdowns to realize that I can't get around him and that he can run rings around me."

We held them on their first series of downs mostly because of their disorganization in adapting to the new rules, and forced them to kick. Each time we got the ball, Jack threw a perfect strike, one of which I dropped. We scored on the other two in spite of the fact that the assistant pro had me covered

40

like a blanket. Jack's passes were so perfect that each time the assistant pro leaped to knock down the ball it was just beyond his reach. Then he was too far off balance to recover fast enough to catch me.

Finally the score was two touchdowns apiece, and we had the ball. A score now meant victory. You have to play with a Kennedy just once to know that victory is what you are out there for even if it is only a short game of "touch" on the first fairway at Pebble Beach. With the prospects of victory in our clutch, Jack was thoroughly enjoying himself. When we came back into the huddle on our series of downs, he said with a rising tone of optimism, "We'll try the perfect Melacreamo."

"What in God's name is a perfect Melacreamo?" I asked.

Analyzing me with a slight look of disgust, he answered: "I'll center the ball to you, then I'll fake as though I'm going down for a pass. But I will come back for a lateral, and you go deep. My man will be too late rushing and your man will rush in to tag you and you'll be gone and clear for a pass."

The play developed exactly as the Senator from the Commonwealth of Massachusetts predicted. He threw another perfect pass right in my arms, running full tilt. I ran in easily for the score.

After thanking our opponents, the next President of the United States walked off that informal playing field pleasantly happy having done what he loved to do in anything he undertook—give his all and win.

CHAPTER SIX

N JULY 9, 1960, my wife and I flew to Los
Angeles, and as soon as we landed we were caught
up in the swirling excitement of the convention.
Joe Kirnell, a friend from PT boat days who was
in charge of transportation for the convention, assigned us a car
with a volunteer driver, a merchant sailor cook named Dave
Barry, to drive us out to Beverly Hills, where we were to stay
with Bob and Ethel and Ted and Joan. Dave, upon learning
that I had been in PT's with his idol, Jack Kennedy, said he'd
try to be assigned to us for at least another day.

The next evening we ran into the candidate as we arrived
at the house where Mr. Joseph Kennedy was staying. I called
Dave over to meet the Senator.

"Senator," I said, "I want you to meet one of your greatest admirers. Dave has had the good fortune to be the volunteer driver for the Bride and me for all of our official responsibilities."

I could see a slightly mystified expression on the candidate's face as he mused on what were the Fays' official responsibilities which required a car and driver. The expression then turned to mock admiration as he turned to Dave.

"Dave," he said, "I can think of few more valuable contributions to the campaign than seeing that Red Fay gets to where he wants to go."

Dave took this as a direct order from the highest authority he recognized and never left our side, which was the exact opposite of the message the Senator had obliquely tried to convey.

Thanks to Bob and Ethel we were billeted throughout the whole convention week in the bathhouse at the home of Marion Davies' sister in Bel Air. This was only a few blocks from Marion Davies' own home, which she loaned to Mr. Kennedy for the convention period. Bob and Ethel, with most of their children, along with Ted and Joan, were up at the main house.

Beggars can't be choosers, but the bathhouse left a little to be desired. There was no heating, so it was very, very warm in the early evening after a hot day and very cold in the early mornings. The plumbing was a little simpler than we were accustomed to, with the sink behind the bar serving as our washbasin. There were no closets for our clothes. There was one bed, which my wife slept in. I slept on one of the couches. We were near the swimming pool, and the drapes on the windows facing the pool could not be drawn. Each morning about 8:30, young Joe, Kathleen and Bobby Kennedy would invariably come down for a dip. We would see their faces at the window as they made a friendly inspection of the bathhouse to see if we were all right.

Our first night in Los Angeles we had dinner with Ethel, Joan, Jean Smith and Mr. and Mrs. Kennedy at their convention home in Beverly Hills. After dinner we had planned—Ethel, the Bride and myself—to go down to Chasen's restaurant, where Jack was supposed to visit at a party given by Phil Regan, the former singing cop, for the United Steelworkers.

Dirty John Galvin rang up just as we were getting ready to leave. "Patty and I are down here at Chasen's as the personal guests of Dave McDonald, the president of the United Steelworkers," Dirty John said. "Dave hasn't had the opportunity to meet us yet, but we're keeping the party moving. But what I'm calling about is that Jack is due here any minute and I think you ought to be here to deaden the impact."

"We'll come right down," I said, "but do you think you can get us in?"

"Redhead, why ask the ridiculous?" John said. "I could even get your friend Gerry Brush in here." (Brush was a friend of mine who didn't appreciate John.) "Come right on down."

In about fifteen minutes we were pulling up in front of Chasen's with Ethel in her limousine. Dirty John was on the curb to greet us, but before he could put into operation the delicate series of steps he had arranged to get us in, some representative of Phil Regan's spotted Ethel.

"Mrs. Kennedy, we're delighted to have you here," he said. "Won't you please follow me?"

44

Ethel delayed him a moment. "I'd like to introduce you to my friends, the Fays and Mr. John Galvin."

The greeter picked up the ball immediately. "We're delighted to have them. Please come in."

While this little exchange was going on, flash bulbs were flashing on all sides. People were pushing and peering to catch a glimpse of each new arrival with the hope of recognizing a celebrity—and Ethel Kennedy was a celebrity.

We pushed our way in, with our greeter leading the drive.

Inside, the din was terrible. There was no doubt that the candidate was here. The flash bulbs in one corner pinpointed his location. Ethel was taken through the phalanx of bodies to sit with the candidate, while my wife and I went with John to join John's wife, Patty. We had no sooner succeeded against heavy odds in getting drinks along with the rest of the freeloaders when a man came up with a look of great urgency.

"Are you Red Fay?" he asked.

I responded in the affirmative.

He continued breathlessly, "The Senator wants you and your wife to come over to his table. Follow me."

Turning to Dirty, I said, "Fall right into line. It will make the Senator feel a lot more confident if he knows you're here."

John grabbed Patty and forged ahead with us. Suddenly we were out of the shadows and into the light. Instead of backs, we saw a wall of smiling faces. The Senator indicated that we should sit down on a leather bench one seat away from him. Then, pulling me forward, he turned to Dave McDonald.

"Dave, I want you to meet Red Fay, a big construction contractor in Northern California."

I could see Dave searching his memory, trying to connect the

45

name and the business. This was just the reaction the Senator desired. He knew McDonald could search every brain cell and still not find the answer. The Fay Improvement Company probably used not more than ten thousand pounds of steel a year.

McDonald couldn't have been more gracious. "Oh, of course, I know the operation well," he said.

Pulled off into another conversation, the Senator soon broke free again. He leaned over to me and in a subdued whisper said, "With the way the liquor is being poured down here, I'm sure that every steelworker must feel this is a sound way to invest his dues."

Almost as suddenly as he had come in, the Senator was on the move again. As he rose to leave, all those who had held back were suddenly overcome with a compulsion to introduce themselves, or maybe just to say, "Jack, I'm with you all the way." He passed through the room to the door, and in a few seconds he was gone. The party began thinning down to the drinkers who were going to make a night of it as long as the wassail flowed.

Finally the day arrived that would tell whether all the sleepless nights, eating on the run, smiling when you would like to growl and the other demands of a political campaign were justified or whether they were a colossal waste of time, money and energy.

By coincidence, at the Memorial Sports Arena where the convention was held, my wife and I were seated next to Mrs. Stuart (Eve) Symington and her two daughters-in-law. Although we had never met before, there was a remote family relationship, since my father's sister had married Stuart Symington's father's brother. We introduced ourselves, but because of the obvious difference in allegiance it was a reserved meeting.

No sooner were we seated than the series of demonstrations began. The one for John Kennedy was worth all the days of campaigning in Wisconsin and West Virginia. After the rising crescendo of enthusiasm came to an end, I felt certain of Jack's victory.

Later came the demonstration for Adlai Stevenson. I thought it would never end. Horns, sirens, whistles could be heard from every section of the balcony. Banners of unbelievable size were spread out and waving wherever you looked. Finally, when the end came, I felt that Jack Kennedy had just been shown up by the old pro—that this was not a game for young men but a contest for the veterans. My wife felt the same way.

I jumped out of my seat and went down on the floor to talk to Larry O'Brien and Kenny O'Donnell. On the way I happened to pass the exit through which most of the Stevenson demonstrators passed to leave the arena. They were standing in line and were getting paid like special guards. I'd never heard of any such arrangement for Jack and was stunned because I thought all campaigning was voluntary, at least on that level.

After I got onto the convention floor, I spotted O'Brien, O'Donnell, Bill Battle and Tom Mason in a circle talking. I broke in. "My God, have you ever seen such a demonstration! Why, it was twice the demonstration put on for Jack." Then I continued, "What can we do to stem the Stevenson tide before he runs away with this nomination?"

O'Donnell, in his usual emotionless manner, stared at me

47

coldly. "Forget the whole Stevenson demonstration," he said. "It means nothing. We've got this in the bag. All we have to worry about is winning the election."

He seemed so completely confident and unwavering in his opinion that he relieved me of most of my anxiety.

I returned to my seat in the balcony to join my wife. I doubt that there were many people in that arena who didn't have a stake in one of the candidates. Eve Symington and her family waited tensely with their talley sheets, their conversation limited to brief exchanges in subdued tones. I'm sure Eve reasoned that if Stuart was ever going to be President of the United States he would have to win now. Any future convention would probably choose a younger man.

It was no less a dramatic moment for us. Now all the years of John Kennedy's preparation had brought him within reach of the prize.

The balloting started.

We had a copy of a sheet that Bob had prepared for Ethel showing how the states would have to go for Jack to win the nomination. We kept matching and totalling as the balloting went along.

By the time Washington had been reached I could see a strong chance for victory on the first ballot if Bob's predictions were accurate.

This was no time or place for a man with a weak heart. The Johnson and Stevenson supporters knew that they could not win unless a second or third ballot was required and desperately hoped to get through the first round safely. Symington's chance lay still further in the future, perhaps after several

48

ballots, when he might be chosen as the compromise candidate to break a deadlock.

The announcement of the Washington vote, followed by the ballots of West Virginia and Wisconsin, unleashed explosions of applause by Kennedy followers. The noise seemed even more pronounced because of the tense silence of the supporters of the other candidates. With Wisconsin's announcement, it was obvious to everybody in the arena who had kept a running count that Wyoming could give the nomination to John Kennedy.

All eyes were focused on Wyoming. There in the middle of the delegation was Teddy Kennedy. "You have in your grasp the opportunity to nominate the next President of the United States," he told them. "Such support can never be forgotten by a President."

An instant later, the head of the delegation announced: "Mr. Chairman, the great State of Wyoming is proud to cast all its fifteen votes for the next President of the United States, John Fitzgerald Kennedy."

The band blared out. Bob and Teddy were mobbed. Kennedy placards and banners waved and bobbed in all directions. The followers of the defeated candidates sat stunned.

Eve Symington and her family got up and squeezed by us to the aisle.

"If Jack couldn't have won, we would have wanted Senator Symington," I said to her lamely.

Understandably, she found it difficult to respond. She did give me a wan smile.

We looked over at the Robert Kennedy contingent. Banners

49

were swinging in all directions. Now and then the body of one of the four children would catapult into a nearby row of seats, the damage fortunately limited by his forty- or fifty-pound weight.

An announcement came from the speakers' platform that the new standard-bearer for the Democratic Party had left his retreat where he had been watching the returns and was on his way down to the convention arena.

Finally word was passed that the candidate was right outside the arena and would be at the rostrum in a few minutes. Then he appeared. As he stepped forward to speak, the whole convention stood up, whistling, applauding and shouting.

Late Thursday my wife and I went over to the Joseph Kennedys' with Ethel and Joan to watch the nomination of Lyndon Johnson on TV. Soon after the convention had nominated Johnson, Jean and Steve, Eunice and Sarge, Pat and Peter arrived along with Frank Sinatra. Teddy Kennedy came in later with Bob. Mr. Kennedy put Frank Sinatra, Peter and myself to work fixing drinks for the gathering.

Word was passed by the butler that Senator Kennedy was driving up into the brick courtyard. We all were gathered in the living room. Unconsciously we had all moved into a large half-circle facing the entrance hall. The candidate suddenly came through the front door into view and started toward us down the long hall with that characteristic gait of his. Without signal or planning, everybody burst into cheers and shouts. I threw in a couple of piercing whistles and got a little support somewhere along the line.

Once he reached the living room, Jack started around the

half-circle, shaking hands with each of us, accepting congratulations and returning some personal remark.

When he reached me, I blurted out, "Senator, you are fantastic."

He looked at me, shook my hand, then glanced down at my shoes. In a faintly lowered tone, he said, "Where did you get those awful orange shoes?"

I couldn't help laughing, because the color of this very pair of shoes had been the subject of a lengthy discussion about four years earlier.

When he first ran for Congress, Jack became convinced that dress was one mark of the successful man. He had most of his clothing tailored in New York, and his suits featured long thin lapels, with two buttons on the coat front. From 1946 on, his increasing interest in his clothing began to influence his friends. This resulted in my spending more money for my clothes, including a pair of brown shoes from Brooks Brothers. No sooner had I made this purchase of about thirty-five dollars' worth of shoe than the Senator arrived in San Francisco.

"My God," he said, "where did you get those shoes? You've got to do something to darken them up. They look almost orange."

"What do you mean?" I said. "I just paid thirty-five dollars for these shoes. They were made in England especially for Brooks Brothers."

"They're good shoes," Jack said patiently. "All you need to do is have them darkened. Give them to me. I've got a fellow back East who can stain them just the right color. It will only cost you about five bucks."

Visualizing the strong possibility that they would end up in a Kennedy closet in either Boston, New York, Washington or Palm Beach, never to be seen again, I declined. But I was so impressed by his argument that I had the shoes darkened to the color of the Senator's shoes. Here, four years later, on the second most important date in his political career, he remembered those formerly orange shoes.

Dinner was delayed because several leaders of the national labor movement were due to stop by. Jack wanted to make sure that he got their endorsement, and had moved fast to get them to come by that evening. When they arrived the family atmosphere changed. Everybody either got back to work or made sure that he didn't interfere with the operation at hand.

From my vantage point, it was fascinating to observe the operation. Here was a meeting of the three major powers in our country: Big Business, Big Labor and Big Politics. The Kennedys were working from a fairly pat hand, with two of the three levers of the power structure in their hands.

The initial greeting was too enthusiastic to be real for people who didn't know each other that well. The union representatives, in spite of their ease of manner, reflected in their faces the tough struggle they had weathered to rise to the top of their organizations.

The meeting lasted about twenty minutes. When they had left, Mr. Kennedy called everybody in for dinner.

I asked Jack, "Was the meeting a success?"

"Not completely. They were very noncommittal."

There wasn't enough room for everybody to be seated.

Joseph Kennedy immediately solved the problem. "Four people will have to eat in the breakfast room."

"Anita and I can eat in there," Ethel volunteered. I could see the disappointment on Anita's face. She wanted to hear every detail of this day in the life of John Kennedy.

Just as that moment, Peter Lawford and Frank Sinatra walked in from the living room where they had been putting away a "rammer" before dinner. Spotting them, Mr. Kennedy barked in a joking manner, "All right, you two bums, in the other room with the girls." Suddenly as far as the Bride and Ethel were concerned the breakfast room was "in"— and "We hope the rest of you have fun."

My seat was next to Jack. He almost always ate as if somebody were about to grab his plate, but tonight it was not unlike a rapid-fire surface excavation. He seemed tense, nervous and easily irritated.

"What do you think the reaction was to Lyndon Johnson's selection for the Vice Presidential position?" he asked. He glanced at me, then at the others at the table.

I could tell how deeply concerned he was with that decision. Jack had won the nomination by vote of the delegates, and was their choice. But Lyndon was his choice. No longer was Jack representing just the State of Massachusetts. Now he spoke for the entire Democratic Party. He had made his first decision as their titular head, a decision which could spell either victory or defeat for the Democrats in November, and he wanted assurance that he was right.

As if he had read Jack's thoughts, Joseph Kennedy asked at almost the same moment from his seat at the other end of the table, "Bill, what do you think of Johnson as the Vice Presidential nominee?"

Bill Battle (later to become U.S. Ambassador to Australia) replied without hesitation: "Lyndon Johnson was the only choice. The only chance of a Catholic getting support in the South is having a ticket which has a Southerner on it. Johnson is a Southerner who is acceptable to the North. I don't think there could have been a better choice."

I could sense immediately the relaxation of Jack's tenseness. He settled back and started to enjoy as much as everyone else the recollection of a hundred little incidents and episodes in the months since he had decided to run for the Presidency.

Lts. (jg) George "Barney" Ross, Paul "Red" Fay and James "Jim" Reed pose with Lt. John "Shafty" Kennedy at Tulagi, Solomon Islands, 1943.

*John Kennedy runs Barney Ross,
Lennie Thom, Jim Reed, Red
Fay and Bernie Lyons through a
dummy scrimmage at Hyannis
Port. Summer, 1944.*

Red Fay, Lennie Thom and friend. Hyannis Port, 1944.

Red Fay, John Kennedy, Lennie Thom, Jim Reed, Barney Ross, Bernie Lyons, Ted Kennedy and Joey Gargan. A gathering of war heroes (?), Hyannis Port, 1944.

Dressed in Navy dungarees, still recovering from his wartime injuries, Lt. John Kennedy smilingly listens to more from Lt. Paul Fay. Palm Beach, 1945.

Lt. John Kennedy, still on the binnacle list, finds himself listening again to junior officer, Lt. Paul Fay.

Lt. John Kennedy suits up for the last time in his Navy uniform before his medical discharge, with two former PT boat shipmates, Lt. Ben Smith and Lt. Paul Fay.

The candidate does not appear to be considering seriously the advice coming his way just before he made his announcement to run for Congress in 1946.

John Kennedy instructing Red Fay on how to conduct himself in Newport society at Bailey's Beach several days before his wedding in 1953.

John Kennedy about to sweep around his right end and Red Fay on the Kennedy playing fields at Hyannis Port several days before his marriage in 1953.

John Kennedy pauses for a moment several days before his wedding in 1953 with his bride-to-be, Jacqueline Bouvier, at Bailey's Beach, Newport.

John Kennedy about to smack a forehand deep to the base line in the forehand corner for a clean putaway. Hyannis Port, several days before his wedding, 1953.

CHAPTER SEVEN

N EARLY AUGUST, John Kennedy's final drive for the Presidency began. Bob Kennedy called from New York to ask me to suggest a chairman for the Citizens for Kennedy movement in Northern California.

"Redhead," he said, "it has to be someone who can give full time, is not too closely allied to either of the parties and is not a controversial figure. I realize I'm giving you the description of a man who probably doesn't exist, and if he does he'd have to be a failure or a real bore, but we need someone close to that description."

"Bob, we've got just the man," I said. "The last thing he

could be accused of is being a bore or a failure; besides, Jack knows him and he is a great admirer of Jack's. His name is John Harllee. He's a recently retired tombstone admiral from the Navy. He is all fired up to do the job. He was a squadron and area commander in PT boats during the war, and worked on a special project for Jack when Jack was a Congressman, dealing with improving the entrance regulations at the different military academies. Ask Jack about him, because he was very much impressed with the job John Harllee did on this project."

"Send me a résumé and I'll check him out," Bob said. "He sounds fine." Then he added: "It would be awfully nice if the San Francisco headquarters could be the first Citizens for Kennedy to open in the nation with Jack's old shipmates, Red Fay and Admiral Harllee, in charge."

We were the first, and our organization grew almost without soliciting support.

Saturday before Labor Day we faced our first big test. The candidate was coming, and could only spend a few hours at the airport for a rally and a fund-raising luncheon before heading up to Alaska. It was a bright, sunshiny day and a happy buoyant crowd came out to greet him. My daughter, Kathy, had cut a bouquet of hydrangeas to give to the Senator.

The candidate's plane taxied up. As soon as the door of the plane opened and the ramp was pushed into place, the crowd broke through our poorly established restraining line, swarming forward, pushing, laughing and shouting, "Jack, Jack!"

Jack stepped out of the shadows of the interior of the plane onto the ramp, setting off a roar of excitement. He walked down the ramp, to be engulfed by the crowd. Finally he got to the platform that had been hastily constructed to provide a place for him to speak. He spoke briefly, then was carried by the crowd to his car.

Kathy tried to give him the bouquet but never got close enough. Finally in desperation she sailed the hydrangeas over the crowd toward Jack, and the bouquet came down in pieces all around him. He turned, caught one of the flowers, and tried to see who had thrown it, but he couldn't turn far enough to see Kathy because of the mob.

Knowing he was going to a lunch for "fat cats" in the private dining room high up in the terminal, I took my children and my nieces and nephews and raced ahead to intercept him as he came off the elevator that would carry him to the dining level. My daughter Sal, who was only four, was beginning to tire, so I picked her up.

Our timing was perfect. As the candidate stepped off the elevator, our entourage surrounded him.

"My God, they're not all yours, are they?" he said to me, knowing they weren't. Focusing on Sally, he asked, "Is this my godchild?" He then did something which was definitely out of character. He took Sally from my arms into his.

Jack could never be classified as a baby-kissing politician. Holding strange babies had about as much appeal to him as having someone put an arm around his shoulders. Once he had Sally in his arms, I could sense almost immediately that he was searching for a way to unload his bundle without offending the father.

Enjoying having the candidate in a situation in which he had momentarily lost control, I pleaded with Sal, "Give your godfather a big love and kiss."

Sal at the moment was exhibiting even more open disenchantment with the predicament than her godfather was. She was straining to get out of his grasp, leaning back in his arms, surveying him with mingled apprehension and suspicion.

Finally, figuring that her only hope of escaping was to carry out her father's wishes, she quickly leaned forward and gave Jack a very slight peck on the cheek. As if both considered that was the signal to disengage, Jack passed Sally back to me, saying, "I don't think the kid—" called so because I'm sure he didn't remember her name—"quite caught that strong quality of love of children so much a part of the candidate's makeup which has made him so dear to the hearts of all mothers."

Before his marriage, Jack seemed completely indifferent to children. When I'd tell him with great enthusiasm of an experience with my children, he'd say, "I don't understand how you can get such a big kick out of your children, particularly when they are only about one and three years of age. Certainly nothing they are going to say is going to stimulate you. You're not going to discuss with them any of the problems down at the plant."

He said it as though he wanted me to convince him that he was wrong. He really wanted to understand why almost all of his friends who were fathers were so crazy about their children.

With the birth of Caroline and John, Jr., he found the answer himself. During the Presidential years, I think he enjoyed himself more when he was with Jacqueline, playing with his children, than at any other time.

At the luncheon that day in California, the candidate made a short speech emphasizing the importance of party unity and the need to wage an intensive and expensive campaign. Ben Swig, a transplanted Bostonian who owns the Fairmont Hotel, then took the floor and in his New England twang said:

"Ladies and gentlemen, Jack has only a short while here. We've got to show him he can count on San Francisco and California. He needs money to run his campaign, and I want to give it to him today. We have to raise a hundred thousand dollars for him now. Who will give me ten thousand?"

I thought he was out of his mind asking for such a contribution, but Mrs. Walter Heller (a powerful Bay area Democratic Party figure) stood up without blinking an eye and passed forward a check for ten thousand dollars.

Ben continued, calling people by name.

"Come on, Henry McMicking, you can give a thousand. Don't let Jack down." Henry gave. (Henry is an old pal of mine, and as one of his many accomplishments is vice chairman of the board of Ampex.)

I looked at the candidate. Reserved by nature, he obviously found Ben's use of him as bait undignified and painful. But he also realized that this was a job that had to be done, and that few were as effective at it as Ben.

Ben called on Dick Barrett, the younger of the brothers who operate the Barrett Construction Company in San Francisco. Dick, a big fellow with a great sense of humor, got to his feet.

"I'd like to give a hundred dollars," he said, "but I'd like an assurance first from Senator Kennedy that if he is elected he won't make Red Fay Secretary of the Navy."

The whole room burst into laughter. The Senator rose with a smile on his face and replied: "You can be assured that not only will Red not be the Secretary of the Navy, but he won't be the Secretary of the Air Force or Army either."

The proceedings continued, with Ben squeezing out contribution after contribution until the Senator had to leave to prepare for his trip to Alaska. Going down in the elevator, he whispered to me, not in a reproachful tone but with obvious relief that the whole thing was over, "Old Ben doesn't waste any of his talents on subtleties. I'm not sure that there isn't a more sophisticated means of raising money. I hope I don't have to go through many more just like this."

Early in his political life, especially during his first race for Congress, Jack suffered from something close to a sense of guilt about taking money for his political campaigns. The vast Kennedy fortune was no secret to anyone, and some supporters found it almost ludicrous to give John Kennedy a contribution. (The feeling of many people was summed up so well by Willard Wirtz, the Secretary of Labor, several years later at a fund-raising party for Bob Kennedy at Secretary of the Treasury Douglas Dillon's home in Washington, D.C., during Bob's campaign for Senator from New York. Standing in the entrance to the living room, facing Washington's elite, Wirtz said, "I wish my dad were alive and here today because otherwise he wouldn't believe it. Me, Willard Wirtz, standing in Doug Dillon's home asking for money for Bob Kennedy.")

After those early races, Jack recognized the necessity of collecting political contributions—not just to avoid getting a reputation for buying his way into office, but because he knew from experience the vast expense of running for major office. Even so, to my knowledge, Jack never reached the point where he himself would actually ask for financial contributions.

His expression of appreciation for political contributions was always genuine. When he started running in the primaries, I gave him a thousand dollars, which was not only my largest political contribution then or since, but sent hot flashes through

60

my hands. He said to me once, "After receiving that Fay grand, I had to ask myself, 'Do I really know Red Fay? Is this the same Red Fay who wrote me two letters demanding the twenty dollars I owed him?' In any case we're not looking back, and have high hopes for the future."

But political campaigns were many more things than fund-raising, and John Kennedy reflected a positive response to them all. His reaction to an opponent was generally one of understanding, until he opposed Dick Nixon for the Presidency. If Kennedy's proposals for helping anti-Castro Cubans were followed, Nixon said, this could cost us all our friends in Latin America, and would serve as an invitation to Khrushchev to interfere in this hemisphere. The result could be World War III, Nixon asserted.

Giving the appearance of cloaking himself with the policy of the Eisenhower administration, Nixon charged Jack with making "shockingly reckless" proposals that could only be the recommendations of an immature man.

Jack could have accepted the criticism, but after the election when he was briefed on the policies practiced in dealing with different countries, he found that in fact it was the policy of this country to support the anti-Castro forces in Cuba, and that this was well known by Vice President Nixon. He was amazed and concerned that anyone with such lack of understanding of the fitness of things could have come so close to being in the most powerful position in this country.

He said with concern, "Nixon wanted the Presidency so bad that there were few extremes he wouldn't grasp for to try to achieve his goal."

Maybe the prize of the Presidency is so great that it is

impossible for the two contestants to ever really develop any sort of a friendship after the battle is over, but in this case the relationship was a 180-degree reversal from what it had been back in the Congressional years when Jack Kennedy wrote me on November 14, 1950: "I was glad to . . . see Nixon win by a big vote."

Six days before the election, the candidate made his final visit to San Francisco to attend a hundred-dollar-a-plate dinner at the Palace Hotel and then make a major speech at the Cow Palace.

When his caravan arrived at the hotel, surrounded by motorcycle police with their sirens wailing and their red lights flashing, he was swept inside the Palace by the crowd. People were pleading for autographs, trying to shake his hand or just trying to touch him.

He was carried from the door to the elevator on a great human tidal wave. I could see it coming. The only way to avoid being swept up by it was to stand hard against the wall. I was in this position when I caught Jack's eye. By pointing up over his head and moving his lips, he indicated that I should come upstairs.

There was a crowd in the hallway outside his door. When I knocked on the door, a big fellow I'd never seen before opened it a crack and asked what I wanted.

"I'd like to see Senator Kennedy. Tell him it's Red Fay."

The big fellow said, "Wait a minute."

When the door shut with me still on the outside, I got that "we told you so" look from the crowd in the hallway. Then Congressman Jack Shelley looked out the door and spotted me. Turning to the man who had opened the door before, Shelley said, "That's Red Fay. Let him in."

Once I was inside the suite, Shelley said, "Go in the bedroom. He's in there."

I found Pierre Salinger, Ted Sorensen and Kenny O'Donnell in conversation there.

"Hi, Redhead," Pierre said, and pointed at another door. "He's in the bathroom taking a bath."

At first I hesitated to go in, but Pierre said, "Go in. I'm sure he is just resting in the tub and would like to see you."

I started in and saw the candidate soaking in the hot water. That handsome face looked drawn but still keen and quick. He called: "Redhead, come on in. This body which so heroically weathered the trials of the great war and has once again answered the call of the campaign trail is taking a good soaking before again responding to the call."

Seeing him lying there relaxed, so completely cut off from the worshiping mob that swirled just a few feet beyond the bathroom door, I couldn't help thinking how many times over the years the campaign pace had been interrupted to accommodate that hot bath for the aching back. It got to mean more than just physical therapy. It also was an escape from the omnipresent political hangers-on. As a general rule, people just don't follow a man into a bathroom.

At the Bellevue Hotel in Boston in 1946, the bathroom was recognized as the inner sanctum. I would often find the candidate relaxed and at ease in the hot tub nursing his back while his advisers and aides were streaming perspiration as they stood there in the steaming bathroom. That hot, soothing, soaking bath seemed to become a fixed part of John Kennedy's routine during the high-pressure campaign he always waged.

Both during those early days and all through his political life, Jack employed another technique to escape the demands of people who could not recognize how many calls were being made on his time. He discovered a means of doing this without offending the people he had to break away from.

Whenever the campaign trail took us to a large milling gathering during that 1946 race, invariably the time allotted would be too short or the candidate would get stuck with one group or another and find it almost impossible to extricate himself gracefully. It was easy to see when he wanted to make the break. Catching my eye, he'd give me a quick blank stare, slightly widening his eyes. This was my signal.

I'd immediately come up and interrupt the discussion, saying in a very disappointed tone, "Jack, I'm terribly sorry but you promised the Brookline Improvement Association that you would be there at 8:30 P.M. and we're already ten minutes late. I'm afraid we have to leave right now."

Then, with me the target of hostile stares from the people gathered around him, the candidate would say, "We'll leave in a few minutes," and go on talking to his group.

In an irritated tone, I'd reply, "We have to go. This meeting has been on our schedule for weeks. Besides, if we stay here any longer it will foul up our whole schedule for the evening."

Then, with a look of frustrated resignation, the candidate would take his leave and depart, still beloved by one and all.

In the hotel bathroom during this final campaign visit to San Francisco, he asked me suddenly, "How do you think the campaign is going out here?"

Being a perennial optimist, I came back, "Fantastic. When you have something to sell, anybody can merchandise."

Shaking his head in mock frustration, he commented, "It's wonderful having your political future in the hands of amateurs." And then he summed up his view of the campaign: "Last week, Dick Nixon hit the panic button and started Ike speaking. He spoke in Philadelphia on Friday night and is going to make about four or five speeches between now and the election. With every word he utters, I can feel the votes leaving me. It's like standing on a mound of sand with the tide running out. I tell you he is knocking our block off." He added, almost to himself, "If the election was tomorrow I'd win easily, but six days from now it's up for grabs."

Then—the only time I ever heard Jack allude to the possibility of defeat—he mused, "Well, Redhead, if we lose we can get ourselves a sailboat and drift through the Greek islands with our beautiful wives administering to us."

Suddenly any thought of possible defeat was behind him. Once again completely enthusiastic about the prospect of victory, he said exultantly, "Tonight I'm going to talk about the Peace Corps."

He went on to describe in detail some of the features of the program. This was "Jack" Kennedy at his best. He saw the Peace Corps as a chance to lift, even if slightly, the burden of poverty and ignorance that oppresses so many peoples of the world. He continued: "It is a conceptual plan. Many of the details will have to be resolved. Possibly it could be an alternative to military service." Then, back in the political mode, he stated, "And you watch, the Republicans will proclaim that it's an eleventh-hour proposal of a desperate man, poorly conceived, purely political and of no substance . . . the immature reasoning of an inexperienced man."

Fired by either the thought of his forthcoming speech or the squeeze of his schedule, he got out of the tub.

He put his right hand out in front of me. It was callous and sore-looking.

"My God, is that from handshaking?" I asked.

He nodded, then added, "My hand is about another glove size larger than normal." Then, tensing his muscles, he said, "With all that handshaking this is probably the greatest right hand in America today." Without notice or warning, he belted me in the chest, knocking me up against the wall. It was a damn good right hand!

CHAPTER EIGHT

ITH THE ELECTION behind us, I left for Switzerland to join my wife and children, who had been over there since September. On the eighteenth of December we all headed for Zermatt for a family vacation. There, on the day before Christmas Eve, I received a wire from my father:

BOB KENNEDY IS GOING TO BE WIRING YOU OFFERING YOU A JOB AS UNDER-SECRETARY OF THE NAVY. YOU HAVE NO RIGHT TO CONSIDER SUCH AN OFFER. YOUR OBLIGATION IS TO THE FAY IMPROVEMENT COMPANY.

On Christmas Eve a wire from Bob Kennedy reached me:

ARE YOU INTERESTED IN THE POSITION OF UNDER-SECRETARY
OF THE NAVY? MUST HAVE A REPLY BY THE FIRST OF THE
YEAR.

Having risen no higher than lieutenant in the Navy, I didn't
have the vaguest idea what the duties or responsibilities of
an Under Secretary were. My closest exposure to the top ranks
of the Navy came in January, 1943, when I encountered
Admiral Ernest King, the Chief of Naval Operations, in a
passageway in Washington, D.C. I never quite recovered. He
had been portrayed as a ruthless perfectionist who would
cheerfully impose a life term for one minor military infraction.
I panicked when I saw him approaching. Rather than simply
doing an about-face and heading in the direction from which
I had come at an accelerated rate, I made a 90-degree turn and
headed for the nearest doorway. The door I chose for my
escape was unopenable. I stood there with my face pressed
against it, hand on doorknob, body at attention, awaiting the
sentence from Admiral King. Finally he passed, probably saying to himself, "My God, what is happening to our Navy if
there are many more like that redheaded ensign trying to open
a bolted door?"

After he passed I continued on my mission, thoroughly convinced that my naval career would be a lot more promising if
I stayed out of Main Navy, the Naval Headquarters in Washington, D.C.

After Bob's telegram reached me, I spent most of that day
talking to Clint Olson, a fellow Stanford graduate, who was
the number two man with the U.S. Embassy in London. Clint,

who was also on a Christmas vacation with his family in Zermatt, was convinced that I would be throwing away the opportunity of a lifetime if I said no to Bob Kennedy's question, and the more he talked, the more convinced I became that he was right.

"Red," he said, "there are men in the United States who would give a fortune if they thought that it would get them the job you've been offered."

I polled the family to discover whether they wanted to leave San Francisco and go back to Washington, D.C., for at least two years. The children were dead set against it, but Anita said, "If you think it is the best for all of us, I'm sure we'll go along."

After 6:30 A.M. Mass on Christmas Day, Anita, the children and I spent most of the day discussing the pros and cons of life in Washington. By dinnertime the entire family was as eager as I was to go to Washington.

That night I wrote Bob Kennedy, outlining my responsibilities to our family business. If I was going to turn this over to someone else, I said, I would have to be convinced that the new job I was taking on justified the move—that I would be in a position of such responsibility that I would be making decisions which would have an effect on the course of my country, and not just be filling a desk.

On New Year's Eve, Bob called: "Redhead, we're not going to be able to wait any longer for your decision. There are about ten people who would like the Under Secretary position. What have you decided?"

"Bob, I'm going to accept," I said, "but I have to break

69

the news to my father, so don't make any announcement. But I want to make it clear that if the business starts to run into trouble I'll have to resign."

"If you accept," Bob said, "you'll have to stay on a minimum of two years."

"I appreciate that," I said, "and my intention would be to stay on for at least two years. But I want an out—that if the business is in real trouble within six months, I can resign."

"All right," Bob said, "but this is an agreement between you and me and no one else is to know." Then, shifting gears, he said, "Come back right away so Bob McNamara can interview you for the job." This comment clearly indicated to me that I had not been offered the job firmly, but was a candidate who still had to be accepted. That was exactly the way it turned out.

"Bob," I said, "the whole family is here for our Christmas vacation. I can't break that up, but I can be back on the ninth."

"You have to make it the eighth. Be back in Bob McNamara's office on that day," Bob said. "Let me know when you'll arrive, and I'll set up the appointment. Happy New Year."

I told my wife and the children. They were elated at the prospect of change. But I still faced the problem of letting my dad know. I placed a phone call to San Francisco, and after several hours got through to my father, who is affectionately called "The Battler." The connection was only fair.

"Battler, I just spoke to Bob Kennedy and I told him that I would accept the job if offered but I wanted your confirmation first."

Those were the last words the Battler acknowledged from Switzerland. "Is this the sort of thanks I get for setting you up in business?" he shouted. "Now that I am in my seventies and

70

hoped that I might take it a little easier, you decide to walk out. As far as I'm concerned you don't give a damn for anybody but yourself. I can tell you right now that if you take that job, you're finished with me. If there is anything left in my estate when I die, you'll get none of it."

He hung up.

I was shattered. My dad had always been the dominant figure in my life. His limitless energy, his drive, his total absorption in business and detail when working, his seemingly constant dissatisfaction with the way the business was going were continuing spurs to me to try to do better. A single compliment from my father meant far more to me than a thousand dollars in commissions. On top of that he had never deprived his family of six of anything, be it travel, education or material desires, even in the depths of the depression, when he was fighting to keep his business alive.

Now I was disturbed, not by the prospect of being disowned—because I felt I could always earn a living—but by a major break with my father, breaking jaggedly his dominance and hold over me, and also creating a breach in a family that had always stood together.

I spent that entire night and the next day drafting a letter to my father explaining my position. Before sending it, I sought out a Catholic priest in Zermatt to ask his counsel. I explained the situation as fairly as I could, maybe even painting my role in a poorer light than I deserved. The priest said that I had my life to live and if I was convinced that this was an opportunity I shouldn't deny my family and myself, I should accept it. I then phoned my father's secretary in San Francisco and dictated this letter:

January 6, 1961

DEAR DAD:

Because of personal ambition and a sense of responsibility to my family and Country not shared by you, and not measured by monetary standards, I am going to accept the Government position.

Whether I have failed you as a son, God and only you will know, but this is not a decision I have made lightly or without counsel and meditation.

After our conversation I fairly placed our opposing positions before the Catholic priest here to see if I was blind to the sins of selfishness and false pride. He decided that I was not, and should take the position.

With everyone I have consulted, even to the extent that I have been called from the States, all have felt I would be turning my back on an opportunity available to few men, which if I refused I would regret for the rest of my life. Whether my position will prove wise or tragic, at least I will have had a small hand in guiding the destiny of my Country. . . .

I do not expect you to understand my reasons for making this decision, as our conversation revealed, but it was not easy, for my entire life you have dominated my every move—but not without love.

As time goes on I hope whatever I do you will accept my decision—anyway, my hand will always be extended.

YOUR SON

The long-distance exchange with my father, including the second call to dictate the letter to his secretary, cost me $280. But when I finally hung up, my conscience was clear. I found peace for the first time in ten days. It is just as much part of this decision to say that my wonderful dad relented totally on his stated position of being through with me. After there was no turning back for me and I was finally sworn in as

72

Under Secretary, he gave me his blessing, and I have a sneaky hunch that he was very proud to have his son as Under Secretary of the Navy—at least that is what his friends have told me.

I left my family in Switzerland on the eighth as Bob had directed, and flew back to the United States. The flight into New York was about an hour late, so I missed my connections to Washington. I called Bob, who held me on the wire while on another he cleared my appointment with Bob McNamara for 8:30 P.M.

"It's okay, Redhead," he said. "Be there at 8:30, and when you finish come on out and stay with us."

I arrived at the river entrance of the Pentagon at the prescribed time. The building seemed vast and strange and very empty. I was directed up the stilled escalators to the office of the Secretary of Defense and right into the presence of the new Secretary of Defense-designate.

I'd met Bob McNamara at the Pacific Union Club in San Francisco several years earlier during an auto industry convention. Henry Ford was honored with a luncheon, and one of the Ford people attending was Bob McNamara, then one of Ford's top executives. McNamara had been extremely affable and quick to laugh, but he didn't seem to fit the role of executive of a large corporation. He appeared too young, socially restless and possibly unsure—at least in the presence of his boss.

There was nothing unsure or seemingly inadequate about the very serious man who greeted me that evening at the Pentagon. In fact, from his manner it was hard to believe that he hadn't been Secretary of Defense for years. He was in shirt sleeves and sat behind his big desk with utter confidence.

From my point of view our interview was far from satisfying. Bob McNamara asked very few questions, and I found myself pushing forth information about myself, to make our meeting something more than a hello and good-bye.

After about twenty minutes of this soliloquy before this coldly serious man, our meeting was concluded when McNamara said, "Stop by to see John Connally, the new Secretary of the Navy-designate, on your way west. He will have to give you his stamp of approval."

I agreed and retired quickly, feeling the whole trip back to the States had been wasted. I told Bob and Ethel about my reaction when I reached Hickory Hill in McLean. Ethel seemed dismayed. Bob seemed slightly surprised but philosophical.

The next afternoon, without having either seen or spoken to the President-elect, I was on my way to Fort Worth. I reached John Connally's stylish offices about 8 P.M. and was immediately taken with the new Secretary of the Navy. He was frank, humorous and interested. We had a discussion in considerable depth ranging over quite a bit of territory.

I was satisfied now that my case had been heard. But my pessimism about nailing down the promised job that had caused me to cross an ocean and two-thirds of a nation was not lessened as I took my leave.

"Red, I'll discuss this all with Secretary McNamara, but I wouldn't sell my business if I were you until you hear from me," were John's final words. Under any interpretation, that couldn't be considered a strong vote of confidence, a reassurance that my talents were about to be recognized and welcomed by the Department of Defense.

To derive some pleasure from my stay in Texas, I took a bus into Dallas and spent the evening at the home of an old college and wartime pal, Tom Rhodes, and his beautiful wife, Lillian. It was interesting but also distressing to me that these two very bright and attractive people had been somewhat swayed by Ted Dealey and his Dallas *Morning News*. It was my first taste of the rationalization of the radical right, with the doctrines modified in this case by the rational minds of two intelligent people.

The next morning Lillian convinced me that anything can happen in Texas. Having arisen at about 6 A.M., she greeted her husband with a breakfast of scrambled eggs and ketchup.

I arrived in San Francisco almost completely convinced that my trip had been futile. I was also unsure about whether I would be welcome. I called my mother to say that I was back and asked, "Am I still welcome in my father's home?"

"Don't be ridiculous, you're always welcome," my mother said. "Your father has accepted the fact that you have the right to make this decision, but thinks you have made a grave mistake. Now if you're not going out for dinner, why don't you dine with us?" I accepted immediately.

Once there, I confided to my dad and mother my personal estimate of my chances of being Under Secretary. "Having seen Bob McNamara and having received John Connally's advice about selling my business, I think I'll be right back here with the Fay Improvement Company."

The Battler was elated. "I wouldn't push this thing if they don't want you," he said. "It's liable to create friction which is unfair to Jack Kennedy."

"Battler, this will be the President's decision, but I assure you I won't take anything less if they won't take me as Under Secretary."

When I left that evening to stay with my sister, Jean, I'm

sure the Battler felt confident that I was back with the Fay Improvement Company to stay.

Convinced myself that the position wouldn't materialize, I was back at the firm the next morning as if I'd never been away. That evening on the way home I decided to stop at the Pacific Union Club with a couple of pals of mine, Jack Warnecke and Tom Sullivan, to take a few minutes in the hot room, swim and shower and maybe drink a cold beer. When I was in the hot room clothed in only a sheet, Chester, the pool and locker attendant, called me. I was wanted on the phone.

"You can take it here on Harry's phone in the massage room if you want," he said.

I picked up the phone and heard a voice that sounded like the President-elect, but since I had been kidded on my exchanges with the new President, I proceeded cautiously. "Hello," I called.

"Is this Red Fay? This is your old pal."

Still not completely convinced, I queried, "Who did you you say it was?"

Faking chagrin, he came back: "My God, don't you even know the voice of the President-elect of the United States?"

"Mr. President, the connection back here is so poor I can barely hear that magnificent voice."

"All right, Lovable," he said, "I can't give you the Under Secretary of the Navy position but you've got the Assistant Secretary of the Navy for Installations and Logistics. Actually this is a better position for someone with a business background. You have the responsibility for all the bases and keeping the Navy supplied." Then, applying a very gentle

76

needle, he said, "With the fantastic record you have compiled for the Fay Improvement Company you can make a real contribution."

Faced with a previously stated commitment not only to my father but also to my family that I would not accept any position below that of Under Secretary, I replied, "Jack, I can't accept anything less than the Under Secretary position. My even considering a governmental position has really caused a crisis out here. My dad's ready to disown me and some of my sisters feel my leaving is the same as killing my father. As a result I told my dad I wouldn't accept anything less than the under-secretaryship." Then, switching to the attack, I continued. "Whatever happened to the under-secretaryship?"

"Bob McNamara doesn't think you've had enough big business experience to handle the complexities of the position." And he said suddenly, "My God, you have more guts. Do you realize that both Teddy and Franklin Roosevelt got their start as Assistant Secretary? Look where they ended up. And now Red Fay is saying it's not a big enough job for him."

Suddenly I realized I was arguing with the President of the United States. "God, I know all that," I said, "but I just can't break faith with my family."

Realizing the deep and lasting disappointment I would feel if I couldn't be part of the New Frontier, I went on: "Mr. President, I think I'm as well suited by background as anyone to do the job. In a big business very few people get the same opportunity for responsibility in all phases of the business as the operator of a small business. With a large firm they are forced to specialize to a degree which is not the case with a small business. From where I sit and what I know about the responsibilities of the Under Secretary as compared to my responsibilities in the Fay Improvement Company, the basic difference is adding about three or four zeroes on the end of the figures I have been dealing with here. Then it is just a matter of judgment."

"I must say you make the similarity between the Fay Improvement Company and the United States Government almost a standoff," Jack said in an amused tone. Then, in an inviting tone: "Well, I expect you back here for the Inauguration. Why don't you come in a few days early?"

Still let down, feeling that I would never get my chance to serve as Under Secretary, I replied, "I don't want to come back if I'm not a member of the team. Everybody else will have a job and responsibility to look forward to, but I will just be back for the laughs."

Then, switching again to the attack, I added, "But I tell you this, Mr. President, if you have me as your Under Secretary, not only will you have a good job done by me but you'll have unquestioned loyalty in the Pentagon."

He thought for a couple of seconds, then replied, "Let me have another talk with McNamara and I'll see what I can do. Okay, Grand Old Lovable, we'll miss you." He hung up.

My only consolation was that I had not abandoned my position with my family. That night I had dinner with Dad and Mother again and told them what had happened. My father's delight was obvious.

"I think it was wrong for Jack to try to persuade you to change your position," he said.

"Battler, I'm not going to take issue with the reasoning or decisions of the President-to-be of the United States," I said.

"He has greater problems than whether Red Fay is to be Under Secretary or Assistant Secretary of the Navy."

When I retired for the evening my view of the world seemed sharply narrowed. The chance to play a small part on the big stage seemed lost.

Sunday—five days before the Inauguration—a special delivery letter arrived, with invitations to the Inaugural Ball and the Inauguration. My dad and mother didn't want to deprive me of the opportunity to go, but realized the temptations I would face once I was back there. I said I still wasn't going. If I wasn't going to be part of the team, I wasn't going to be a hanger-on.

The Battler was elated.

CHAPTER NINE

HE MORNING AFTER I had decided not to go to Washington for the Inauguration, I went down to the office about 7 A.M. There I found a wire from the President-elect asking me to be his special guest at the Inauguration and view the Inaugural Parade from the Presidential reviewing stand.

After that, I realized I would be out of my mind not to go back there. How many times do you have a close friend inaugurated as President of the United States? Position or no position, if he cared enough to wire me to come, I was going.

I grabbed the phone to make a reservation to leave by jet, then called Bob Kennedy to say I was coming. "Redhead, you can stay out here with us," he said. "Let us know when you arrive and we'll come down and pick you up."

I rang up my dad and told him I was going on the noon plane. He accepted the news calmly, as if he had known it was coming all the time. By noon, I was on the jet headed east.

After an overnight stay in Chicago with Dirty John Galvin, I reached Washington, D.C., on January 17, and was picked up by Ethel Kennedy, half hidden in the midst of six children, most of them her own, and several happily slobbering dogs. There was a minor problem of finding room for this traveler, solved, if I remember correctly, by me taking either a child or a dog on my lap. It probably was a child. The dogs were too big for me to handle and had a real breath problem.

Out at Hickory Hill in McLean, Bob's and Ethel's home was very much like Grand Central Station. Understandably reluctant to call the President-elect, with all his new responsibilities and obligations, everybody seemed to turn to Bob. The phones, all four lines, rang continuously. It was not unusual to see all four buttons on the phone light up, pick up the phone and discover that a future Cabinet officer or ambassador had been patiently waiting, sometimes for ten or fifteen minutes, to get Bob's ear.

Hickory Hill was also the center for all the pals, campaign workers and newspaper people. It was always good to be sure that you knew who you were talking to before telling the "family secrets," because your words might possibly be in print the next day.

That night was my first exposure to the unbelievable excitement that John Kennedy gave to the Presidency. His sister, Jean Smith, and her husband, Steve, were giving a dinner

81

dance for the President at their Georgetown home. Bob, Ethel and I drove down in their big black Cadillac limousine. The traffic was moving very slowly, and the sidewalks were jammed with people. We pulled up across the street from the Smiths' house to a chorus of shouts: "It's Bobby Kennedy! It's Bobby Kennedy!"

The police tried to hold back the crowd. We were almost blinded by flash bulbs and floodlights as we stepped from the car. Several people ran up to shake Bob's hand, others to seek his autograph. I liked the small part of the limelight that spilled over onto me, but was very conscious of the fact that if I lost a step or got cut off, I would very quickly become a part of the crowd myself. Then I'd be faced with the problem of passing the different "check points" to get into the party.

The house was filled with celebrities. Every place I looked there was someone I had seen either in the movies, on television, on the stage or in the newspapers.

The President-to-be arrived, flashing that handsome smile but also displaying that slight uneasiness he felt at a social gathering. This was, I'm sure, based on the fear that he might be trapped by people he didn't especially want to talk to. He moved along, greeting those who crowded up to greet him until he settled with a group he liked.

I was at table number one. On my right was the beautiful Ginny Tydings, the wife of Joe Tydings, the son of former U.S. Senator Millard Tydings. On my left was Gene Kelly's wife, Jeanne, and on her left was the President-elect. Frank Sinatra and Nat King Cole's wife, Maria, were across the table.

After dinner, the President-elect asked Jimmy Durante and

82

Nat King Cole to sing. When they finished, the President-elect leaned over and said to me, "I think the crowd is ready for a little 'Hooray for Hollywood.' "

He was referring to a song Barney Ross had taught me during the PT boat days in the South Pacific. Barney had trained me to sing it, roughly in the style of Johnnie "Scat" Davis. Whenever there was a holiday or occasion to celebrate out in the Solomon Islands, Barney and I would throw together the ultimate in amateur show business for the squadron or base personnel, and invariably the backbone of the show would be our rendition of "Hooray for Hollywood."

Jack often saw these shows and developed an amused affection for the song. I don't think it was the music or the showmanship that accounted for his fondness. He liked to see the reaction of the audience, particularly if the members were undergoing their first exposure to Ross and Fay. He had Barney and me go through our treatment of this classic up at the Cape when we came home from overseas in 1944, and again me alone at the annual New Year's Eve black-tie party at the Everglades Club in Palm Beach a few months later.

I was hardly seated at the Everglades Club before Jack observed, "What this party needs is Red Fay singing 'Hooray for Hollywood.' "

In stark horror I shook my head to indicate complete disagreement, but Eunice betrayed me. "Red," she said, "that is the sort of thing they love down here. Jack is absolutely right. It would make the difference."

Jean joined in. Only Mr. Kennedy reflected the true reaction, looking at me as though he felt I would be out of my mind if I let them talk me into it.

83

Three thousand miles from home, an unknown, on New Year's Eve, before Palm Beach's *crème de la crème* of society, Red Fay found himself before the microphone and about three to four hundred shocked patrons. As I write this, twenty years later, I still feel the embarrassment of that evening.

I boomed out over the mike, "Ladies and gentlemen, it is my great pleasure to now sing for you one of the great American classics."

Out the words came:

> Hooray for Hollywood . . .
> That screwy-bally-hooey Hollywood,
> Where any office boy or young mechanic
> can be a panic
> with just a good-looking pan,
> And any barmaid
> can be a star maid
> if she dances with or without a fan. . . .

I yelled the lines out—which is the only way I knew how to sing them—and at the same time ran my eyes over that crowd. Most of the people there were obviously stunned. "Can this be happening at our Everglades Club?" I'm sure they were asking themselves. The only thing that kept me from being tossed out bodily was my naval uniform.

Then I looked over at the Kennedy table. Eunice and Jack were laughing so hard they were crying. Jean looked as though she were worrying for my safety. The rest were enjoying Jack's and Eunice's total submission to laughter.

When I concluded my offering, a few polite claps from the

crowd were lost in the applause from our table. Although Jack and Eunice called for an encore, I knew I was lucky to get off without a reprimand from the club president.

When I returned to the table, Jack, still laughing, said, "Even if we're not allowed back in here next year it was worth every minute of it. I feel confident that 'Hooray for Hollywood' will never be sung again in this capitalistic gathering place with quite the same disregard for restraint. Barney would have been proud of you."

Now, as President-elect of the United States, John Kennedy was obviously looking forward to the prospect of watching another roomful of stunned faces.

"Are you out of your mind?" I said as he urged me to perform. "Can't you see me trying to follow probably the two greatest entertainers in show business?"

Almost as if it was planned ahead, Teddy came over and said, "Red, we've got to grab this party before it dies and give them a few renditions of some of those national favorites of yours."

With the warm pleasure that one friend seems to always have for another who seems destined to make a fool of himself in a private gathering, the President-elect locked forces with Teddy.

"For God's sake what are you worried about?" he asked. "If I ever saw a crowd ready for Red Fay, this is it."

Realizing I had no out, I tried to get away with a half-commitment. "All right, I'll get up and introduce Teddy in his interpretation of the Charleston. There is no equal on this continent when he turns it on. But can't you just see the ex-

85

pression on everybody's face when this redheaded unknown suddenly appears on a microphone following Jimmy Durante and Nat King Cole?"

Nothing would stop either of them now. "All right, I'll do the dance and I'll get Claude Hooton to sing 'Heart of My Heart' with me," Teddy said. "Then Red can finish off with a few 'Hoorays for Hollywood.' "

The more I listened, the worse it sounded.

"The introduction is all I do," I said. The President-elect gave me a questioning look that seemed to say, "I hope this is not indicative of the Western interpretation of the spirit of the 'New Frontier.' "

I got up, asked for a chord or two from Lester Lanin, and started in on the introduction of Teddy. I was dead right. The look of amazement on the faces around the room was the complete cincher that there would be no 'Hooray for Hollywood' tonight. Even Teddy had to admit after Claude and he had belted out one of their best songs it did not bring the house down. People were having too much fun just getting to know each other.

Before the President-elect left he said to me, "Red, I haven't had a chance to really get down to it yet with McNamara, but we'll work out something for you on the Navy job."

As I was sleeping in Bob's dressing room at Hickory Hill, I was up with the arrival of the first contingent of children seeking out Bob to settle an argument or childhood crisis that only a dad has the answer to. That morning I reached the breakfast table about five minutes after Bob. Seated at the table with him was a blond, vital, restless man just a little under six feet, who later I was to find out was not only one of Washington's

86

ablest writers but a great favorite with the ladies wherever he went. "Red, I want you to meet Rowly Evans," Bob said. "Rowly, Red Fay."

Since I was not then an avid reader of the editorial page, the name meant nothing to me.

Bob and Rowly continued their conversation. Somewhere in the middle I added my contribution at what I thought was an appropriate time. As Rowly and Bob had seemed like close friends of long standing, my comments were free and uninhibited.

When Rowly finally left, Bob said, "Listen, Red, when you have a newspaperman present, use a little judgment in what you say. Things you say here look an awful lot different when you see them in print."

"Bob, I had no idea who Rowly Evans is or what he does, and still don't."

With a look of mild disgust, Bob replied, "Evans is a syndicated columnist."

On Wednesday night Vice President-elect Lyndon Johnson was the guest of honor at a reception at the Statler Hilton. Bob felt that he and Ethel should make an appearance. I was included, and we headed down.

When we arrived at the side entrance of the Hilton, Bob was greeted with the same enthusiasm as the night before. We were ushered into a small room off the main reception room. The Vice President-elect and Lady Bird were greeting some of their personal friends and members of their family before going out to the receiving line.

This was my first meeting with Lyndon and Lady Bird. I was

surprised because Lyndon was so tall, and surprised also because Lady Bird's pictures hadn't done her justice. She was both very gracious and very attractive-looking.

Their friends, although more than affable, were dressed as if the gusher had just come in. Obviously, the wives had been given the "all clear" at Neiman-Marcus and told that the sky was the limit.

Thursday night was the Gala. Organized by Frank Sinatra with such stars as Ethel Merman, Nat Cole, Jimmy Durante, Gene Kelly, Tony Curtis, and his wife, Janet Leigh, Fredric March and others, it was heralded by entertainers as potentially the greatest variety show ever pulled together.

By 4 P.M. that afternoon, the snow which had been falling since the morning covered the ground. Softly, silently, it laid a deep blanket over Washington. Within hours almost eight inches had fallen. The whole city was suddenly locked in a mammoth traffic jam. In Washington, where social engagements have an aura of importance unequaled in any other city, tempers were rising steadily as very important people tried to meet their commitments. The Gala, scheduled for 9 P.M., was rescheduled for 11 P.M.

For those who braved the storm—and there were many—there was an air of camaraderie that only comes through succeeding where others failed. Bob, Ethel and I drove down with Bob at the wheel. (Ethel's family had commandeered his limousine and hadn't returned in time, probably because of the snow.)

Ethel told me, "I hope you are going to constantly be thinking of things you can do for old Eth because I have really got a prize for you when we get to the Gala. That is, if we ever get to the Gala."

Once we reached the canopied entrance, we turned the car over to a parking attendant and headed in. Bob's and Ethel's arrival was greeted by cheers and shouts. People crowded in from all sides wishing him well, grasping for a hand or sticking out a piece of paper for an autograph.

Inside the gigantic hall, Ethel said, "Before we go up to the box, I got something down here that I want to give to Red." Winding our way through the different boxes, I spotted the movie star, Angie Dickinson, wrapped in fur, standing all alone. Before I could open my mouth, Ethel said to me, "If she'll have you, here is your date for the evening."

As I told my wife later, it was all in the line of duty, an explanation which has never really caught on.

Our box was right next to the Presidential box, and caught the overflow of Kennedys and their friends. Besides Bob and Ethel, Angie and myself, there were Chuck and Betty Spalding, Senator Ben and Sis Smith, Jean and Steve Smith, and others. We weren't settled long when the word was passed that the President-elect and the First Lady-to-be were arriving. This was to be my first occasion to see John Kennedy enter a public place as President-elect.

You could hear the roar of approval of the crowd outside as the President-elect and the First Lady-to-be arrived. Like advance messengers, different people would rush ahead to exclaim, "The President is coming," until finally he and Jacqueline arrived. He seemed to have a wave and smile for everyone as he slowly crossed the ten or twelve feet to his box. As he took the first step down, he spotted me and gestured to me to take the few steps to where he stood.

In the excitement of the occasion, I had a feeling something momentous was going to be said when I reached the President.

He leaned over with what would have to be considered a sly grin and asked, "I wonder if the Bride and Angie will grow to be good friends?" He then stepped down into the box before I could reply.

I'm sure he had accomplished his mission with some delight as he noted the look of anxiety that must have ever so briefly crossed my face.

At the conclusion of the Gala, the President-elect paid a special tribute to Frank Sinatra. Amid the clapping someone said in a subdued voice to me and others close around, "I hope Sinatra will live up to the public image the President has given him by such recognition."

After the Gala, Joseph Kennedy took over Paul Young's Restaurant for a supper dance. As I walked in with Angie, I was greeted by Mr. Kennedy, who barked with no intent to bite, "Wait until I tell your wife how you are conducting yourself." Then, without missing a comma, he turned to Angie, "How are you, dear? You look lovely. Why are you wasting your time with a bum like this fellow?" With a friendly wave he sent us into the room so as to greet the next guests.

About 4:30 A.M. the President came over to the table where Gene and Jeanne Kelly, Nat and Maria Cole, and Angie and I were seated. After a few words to the group he turned to me. "Step out here with me," he said. He led me into the pantry just off the kitchen. Out of earshot of the others, he said with emphasis, "Have you ever seen so many attractive people in one room? I'll tell you Dad knows how to give a party. But while I'm being generally the beloved President-elect, Grand Old Lovable is conducting one of the smoothest operations I've ever seen and is going unnoticed."

Before I could defend myself, he started into the room saying, "I'm going home and leave this all to you." With that the man who the next day would be the President of the United States left the pantry of Paul Young's Restaurant.

The next morning was the great day. Bob had secured a seat for me on the platform six or seven rows behind the President. We drove down by limousine in bright clear sunlight magnified by the reflection of the snow. At the Capitol, it was exciting and exhilarating to walk along with men I had read about but had never been close to before, such as Adlai Stevenson, Douglas Dillon, Dick Nixon, and others. I kept wanting to say hello, because everyone looked so familiar, but the unknowing return stares stopped me.

As the ceremony began, in my opinion the chance for the Catholic clergy to leave a favorable impression with the broad American public upon the election of the first Catholic President was shattered by Cardinal Cushing. He went on and on in an endless monotone as though he had been plugged into the wall and wouldn't stop till somebody disconnected him. Then, after the warm and appealing appearance of Robert Frost, came John Kennedy. Those twelve or thirteen minutes he required to deliver his Inaugural brought excitement and optimism not just to America but to the world. When John Fitzgerald Kennedy turned away from the lectern and walked as President of the United States up the stairs into the Capitol, there was no one in that gathering who didn't sense a new vigor and strength flow into a government and its people.

When we got back into Bob's limousine and turned up Pennsylvania Avenue for No. 1600, then drove through the open iron gates, I felt almost as though I were joining in a masquerade.

I had been in the White House once before on a guided

91

tour. On this second visit, I couldn't help feeling like a trespasser who at any minute might be escorted from the premises. The foreign feeling soon left as I began to see people I'd worked with in Wisconsin, West Virginia, Los Angeles and San Francisco. With Larry O'Brien, Kenny O'Donnell, Chuck Roach, Ted Reardon, Ted Sorensen and Dirty John Galvin around, the White House suddenly seemed to be home base.

While I was enjoying the excitement of the parade, a Secret Service man came up and inquired, "By any chance are you Mr. Paul Fay, Jr.?"

I replied in the affirmative.

"The President would like to see you," he said, and led me down to the front row of the reviewing stand. When the President turned and saw me, he said, "Come on up here, Red," then returned briefly to finish his conversation. When he had completed it, he turned to Lyndon Johnson, who was standing on his left.

"Lyndon," the President said, "I want you to meet the new Under Secretary of the Navy."

I was dumfounded—and elated beyond measure.

Then, turning to me, the President added in a low voice, "If he gets by the FBI." That was how I was notified of my appointment.

CHAPTER TEN

NAUGURAL BALLS WERE being staged at almost every hotel in Washington. Fernando Parra, Kim Novak, Angie and I decided to follow the President as he visited each of the celebrations.

He was going to each of the balls, including the huge one at the Armory. Because of the snow, the traffic in the area was backed up for blocks. The four of us deserted our car and raced through the snow and the slush.

Fernando and I sometimes carried the girls, a challenging undertaking because of the unsure footing.

The President had a police escort to take him from ball to ball. When he moved, he moved fast and without any hindrances, so we had to run to keep up with him. It wasn't until we reached the Statler Hilton, his last stop, that he even realized we were part of his entourage.

With his entrance there, the band played "Hail to the Chief," bringing cheers from the dancers as they surged up around the bandstand. When they quieted down, the President greeted them with a word of appreciation and a statement of optimism for the future.

"There's only one feature of this ball I don't like," he said. "The minute I arrive the music stops and I never get a chance to dance."

Almost every woman in the room raised a hand and pleaded "Me, me!" to assure him he could find a partner. Watching all this from behind the bandstand, partially shielded by the potted palms, were Angie, Kim Novak, Fernando and myself. Angie and I had moved a little forward to get a better view, not realizing that we would be seen by the President. Before we could retreat or escape, he spotted us and walked around the bandstand and right to us. About ten or twelve photographers and commentators were recording his every move. Flash bulbs were popping from all directions.

He said to me in a low voice, "As you stand here confidently basking in the appreciative glow of Hollywood's beautiful film star, Angie Dickinson, the hum of cameras recording every loving emotion, I estimate it will take less than twenty-four hours before the Bride will be able to enjoy this same intimate moment in the Swiss papers."

Suddenly I could see my lovely Bride, alone over in Switzerland, with visions that her husband was living it up with a

94

screen siren. I attempted to put a little distance between Angie and myself until the cameras stopped grinding, to the obvious delight of the President. He soon returned to the front of the bandstand for his final good-bye to the crowd, and then hurried out and down the stairs. Just before he passed through the hotel door to his car, he directed a Secret Service man to summon me. I reached him just as he entered his car.

"Why don't you jump in here and come out to Joe Alsop's with me?" he asked.

"It's great with me," I said. "Is it all right if Angie comes along with us?"

"Fine, but let's get out of here."

Then, feeling a sense of obligation to the rest of the foursome, I added, "Kim Novak and Fernando Parra are also with us. Can they come along, too?"

The President looked at me with rising impatience because of the delay occasioned by my wanting to expand the party.

"I can just see the papers tomorrow," he said. "The new President concludes his first day speeding into the night with Kim Novak, Angie Dickinson, architect Fernando Parra and an old shipmate." With a tone of resignation and a trace of loneliness he said, "Well, Redhead, for a moment I almost forgot that I was President of the United States. It has its advantages and its restrictions, and this is one of the latter. Good night."

The door closed and a young life-loving man sped off into the night, having made his first minor sacrifice to the high office he held.

Angie and I walked slowly back to the dance floor for a

dance, still very conscious of the excitement that had been ours for the few moments when the President of the United States had sought us out.

On Saturday afternoon, January 21, the Cabinet was scheduled to be sworn in at the White House. Jim Reed and I went over together. The Marine Band played softly in the main entrance while well-known public figures arrived and talked quietly, waiting for the President.

We were all directed to the East Room. There the President and his Cabinet assembled officially for the first time. They stood in a semicircle, with their backs to the South Lawn.

I was appalled by the conduct of the working photographers. They had been asked to stand back so that the families and friends of the Cabinet officers could see the proceedings. Instead, they crowded forward so it was all but impossible for the guests to see the swearing in or hear the President's comments. I realized that Mrs. Earl Warren was unable to see her husband administer the oath of office. I asked several of the photographers to step back so Mrs. Warren and her children and grandchildren could see. Finally, Pierre Salinger, seeing that things were getting somewhat out of hand, stepped forward and decisively directed them back to where they had originally been asked to collect.

The oath of office was administered. The President made a few remarks, and then asked that all wives and children of the new Cabinet officers come forward to join their husbands or fathers. Then the other guests were invited to come through the line to congratulate the new officers.

After congratulating Bob Kennedy, Bob McNamara and several others, I came to the President. Before I could say a word he said, "The way you have been conducting yourself all week, I want you to go to church with me tomorrow. Be here in time to go to eleven o'clock Mass." Then he pushed me along the line. That sharp needle which never brought blood or left a bruise had done its job again.

Sunday morning at 10:30 I was at the White House, waiting for the President at the south entrance, just inside the building. About 10:50 he came striding in with that very special gait of his. When he got to the car, I stood aside so the President could enter. He seated himself behind the driver, and I jumped into the seat on his right. As we left the White House grounds by the west gate, a gathering of a hundred or so cheered as we passed through. Strangely enough, most of them seemed to be peering in on my side of the car and those who didn't spot the President next to me seemed a little perplexed. Being a friendly soul, I happily waved back.

"I hope this strong display of affection for the new Under Secretary of the Navy is in recognition of his lovable image and doesn't in any way reflect an early waning of support for the new President," the President said.

Bill Greer, the Secret Service man who was driving, volunteered: "Mr. President, if you will excuse my overhearing you, I believe the rather bewildered look on the faces of some of the people we have passed is caused by the way you and Mr. Fay are seated. It is customary for the President to sit on the side away from the driver, so he can get in and out of the limousine fastest."

That was the last time I ever made that mistake. After I was installed as Under Secretary in the Pentagon, where the military are so protocol-conscious, it amused my wife that I always insisted on having my seat of honor. I must admit I liked that faint trace of prestige that protocol provided.

On our way to Mass, the President asked Bill to drive by his old house on N Street in Georgetown. I'd never been there, and was looking forward to seeing it. As we drove up, the President said in an exasperated tone, "Look at those newspapers piled up all over the front step. I told them to cancel all deliveries out here. I can just hear some of my good Republican neighbors delighting in spreading the story, 'How can he run the country if he can't organize his own home?' " Then he said to Bill Greer, "Bill, stop the car in front of my house."

Before any of us knew what was happening, the new President of the United States was out there picking up the old newspapers and pitching them onto the floor of the limousine with considerable irritation. He finished the job before any of us could move, and his mood improved immediately.

Without knocking or ringing the bell, he pushed open the door of the house next door, waved for me to follow, and marched in calling, "Isn't there anybody in this house who is going to greet the President of the United States?"

Suddenly the beautiful Tony Bradlee, wrapped in her bathrobe, came rushing into the hall followed by her husband, the writer, Ben Bradlee.

"Mr. President, what are you doing here?" she asked. Ben and Tony were having a leisurely Sunday morning breakfast and had not expected to greet the President of the United

States. We stayed for a few minutes and had a cup of coffee. Two of the Bradlee children, both of grammar school age, came running in with a problem that only Mom could settle. They ignored the guests until Tony pointedly said, "Children, will you please remember your manners? Please greet the President of the United States and Mr. Fay."

They chorused, "Good morning, Mr. Kennedy. Good morning, Mr. Fay," and then went right back to their real objective, seeking a solution from Mom. To them the President was still Mom's and Dad's good friend, Mr. Kennedy, who lived next door.

At Mass in Georgetown, a large crowd had gathered to greet the President. The moment he made his appearance they broke into cheers.

The pastor walked forward, offering an overly warm two-handed handshake to the President. You could almost feel the President pull away. He masked his feelings through a somewhat strained smile. John Kennedy didn't like people putting their hands on him, even if it was only a prolonged two-handed handshake.

Inside the church, it was impossible to pray or concentrate on the Mass. It was equally impossible for most of the people to keep their eyes off the President. Some would boldly stare. Others would peep every thirty seconds or so. Some would pretend they were searching for something or someone else, and that their glance just happened to light upon John Kennedy during their search.

Regardless of where they were seated in the church, during Communion most of the people en route to and from the rail managed to swing past the President. In all candor, if I hadn't been with the President I would also have been a peeper or a starer.

I noticed at collection time that the responsibilities of the Presidency had not changed John Kennedy's habits. As usual, he was penniless. He leaned over to me and whispered, "Slip me at least a ten. I want them to know this is a generous President."

I also noticed his whimsical look that told me that I was bidding farewell to my ten dollars.

Teddy Kennedy joined us after Mass and we drove back to the White House. When we got out of the limousine and started through the lower floor, the President asked, "How would you like to see my office over in the Executive Wing?" We both leaped at the chance and followed him out to the pillared walkway which bordered the Rose Garden and led to the President's office.

Obviously the President enjoyed the excursion as much as Teddy and myself. The doors leading to the offices near his were all closed and almost unidentifiable as to whether they were private offices or Cabinet rooms because of the reflection of the garden—the outside—on the glass. In the President's office were only two couches and what must have been President Eisenhower's desk and chair. There were no pictures on the walls.

If there was anybody else in the Executive Wing on this January Sunday morning, they were unheard and unseen. It was almost as if the mighty machinery of the government had come to a halt for one day. I guess because of the time and place we found ourselves speaking in subdued tones.

Sitting down in the swivel chair behind the desk, Jack spun around in it and then looking up, asked, "Paul, do you think it is adequate?"

Looking at him and at the silent closed doors, still hardly able to comprehend that my old pal was in fact the President, I replied, "I feel any minute now that some guy is going to stick his head through one of those doors and say, 'All right, you three guys—out of here.'"

After a brief swing through Evelyn Lincoln's office, we headed back to the Mansion and the second floor where the President lived. Although I had not noticed the Secret Service men while we were walking to and from the Executive Office, it was quite apparent that we had not been beyond their surveillance at any time during our excursion. As we came along the walkway by the Rose Garden, signals were passed ahead so that the elevator up to the living quarters would be waiting.

All or almost all of the Eisenhower furniture was gone, and I could see evidence already of the exquisite taste of Jacqueline Kennedy. Her appreciation of painting, sculpture, and furniture had aroused the President's curiosity, and he was fast becoming a student of the arts himself.

As he took us on a guided tour, we found Jacqueline and several members of her White House Historical Association discussing the selection of different pieces to go in certain locations. We were introduced, but neither the President nor I said much, because most of their conversation was carried on in French in deference to the French museum curator.

The President then began showing us the new paintings on the wall. "Those two are Renoirs and that is a Cézanne," he told me. Knowing next to nothing about painters or paintings, I asked, "Who are they?"

Aghast, the President stepped within a few inches of me and in a shielded whisper said, "My God, if you have to ask a question like that, do it in a whisper or wait till we get outside. We're trying to give this administration a semblance of class. Renoir and Cézanne just happen to be about the two best-known French Impressionist painters."

The guided tour moved quickly into another room. Out in the long hall that divides the second floor, the President started to look through a series of pictures. They were magnificent water colors depicting American Indians driving buffaloes, a buffalo kill by a brave, and several portraits of great chiefs of the past.

Standing off to appraise about six of them, he turned to me. "What do you think?" he asked. "I want to hang a couple of paintings of American Indians in my office. If I don't get them over there right away I'm sure Jackie is going to claim them for this hall. Which do you like best?"

We both agreed on two, one a portrait of a majestic chief and the other of a buffalo herd under attack by Indian hunters. Jack ushered me off to his office with the two pictures. As I walked down the passageway from the White House proper to the Executive Wing carrying two pictures to be hung in the office of the President of the United States, I thought, "Is this Red Fay?" On one hand I was like any ordinary American, giving a friend a helping hand on moving day. On the other hand I was carrying pictures for the President of the United States, pictures to be hung in his office which would become a part of his image to the world.

I entered his office unnoticed and deposited my cargo. It was an unreal feeling to be alone in the office of the President of the United States. It was almost as if for a brief moment in history the engineer had left the control panel and I could throw some imaginary switch which would change the course of our country and the world for all time. This was fantasy, of course, but I did leave two paintings for the President that hung in his office during the entire period in which he was President.

CHAPTER ELEVEN

FTER THE PRESIDENT informed me that I was to be Under Secretary of the Navy, the Justice Department and the Navy Security Department made exhaustive searches into my background and activities to determine whether I should be entrusted with top secret information.

I was not being paid while awaiting clearance. After several weeks had passed and I still had received no word, I telephoned Bob Kennedy to find out what was taking so long.

"Bob," I said "could you check up on my security clearance to see what the delay is? If Grand Old Lovable is not going to get cleared, break it to me quickly before I go broke."

"Let me check into it and I'll call you back," he said.

A few minutes later he was back on the phone.

"Redhead, I've got it all here." Then in jest he continued, "It seems they must have done a very careless job, because they haven't found out how consistently you have dropped the ball." Then, in an interested tone: "You might be interested to note that one of your neighbors doesn't think you are the great figure that we all know and love. She told the agent that you seemed to be frivolous, gave loud, noisy parties and your general decorum was not that of a man who should be put in a position of great responsibility."

By doing a little sleuthing of my own, I later found out who my detractor was. It was a neighbor who had been overly solicitous of us over the years, often asking us to cocktail parties and dinners even though we did not reciprocate with the same enthusiasm. Thanks to the wholehearted support of such old friends as Gardiner Mein, Warren Spieker and Dick Cahill, I was able to weather her unfavorable report.

Finally the clearance came through, and a date was set for my appearance before the Senate Armed Services Committee. I asked the President if there was anything in particular I should be prepared to comment on or any special statement I should make before the committee. He did not foresee any problem that would require comment, but made one suggestion.

"Ask Clair Engle to present you to the committee," he said. "As you're from California and he wasn't consulted on your appointment, it would be a very wise political move, and I think he would be more than pleased to present you."

Senator Engle and I had never met, but he could not have been more helpful and willing. He asked for some biographical

105

information and then requested that I meet him at his office about ten minutes before the committee was scheduled to convene. We could walk over to the committee chambers together.

When the day arrived, the committee room was packed. I had the feeling that a lot of people wanted to be in at the kill. The number of naval officers present was rather sobering too. I wondered if they had been sent up by the Big Man in Blue to get an evaluation of the behavior of the new Under Secretary under fire.

Mr. Frank Ellis was presented to the committee first, and the Senator from Louisiana read his biography. When the Senator finished the presentation, I wondered why Frank Ellis wasn't President of the United States. I'd never heard such a string of accomplishments.

Then Mr. Ellis spoke for himself. I was impressed by his enthusiasm and his ambitious plans for meeting all the challenges of his new post. The more he talked, dealing brilliantly with all the issues, the worse I felt.

The biography I had given to Senator Engle seemed without accomplishment by comparison. It indicated that I was born, got through grammar school, high school and college— not without a definite test of the flexibility of our educational system—served in the Navy, and then went to work for my dad.

I looked over at Senator Engle. He seemed unperturbed about the approaching challenge. Finally, Senator Richard Russell, chairman of the committee, said, "Senator Engle, I believe you have a nominee to present to this committee. Please proceed."

After the fantastic performance that preceded ours, I felt

106

sorry for Engle—but only until he opened his mouth. He started in with one of the great eulogies of all time. The more I listened, the more certain I was that he had grabbed somebody else's résumé.

"Mr. Chairman, not only did Mr. Fay have an illustrious war record, but he stands as one of the great citizens of the great city of San Francisco. His unselfish contribution to civic endeavor . . ." and on and on.

I leaned toward the Senator to see if I could get a glimpse of the source of all this fantasy. I discovered that he had no manuscript. He was making all this up as he went along. Finally I heard him say, "Mr. Chairman, fellow members of the Armed Services Committee, it is my privilege to present to you Mr. Paul B. Fay, Jr."

Seated at one end of the long committee table, flanked on both sides by distinguished Senators, their eyes all focused on me, I felt a sudden panicky urge: "Make a run for it."

I suppressed the urge, and a few minutes later I realized that I had passed the test, not without a great assist from Stuart Symington, and was now about to be officially named Under Secretary of the Navy.

The transition from my former life to Under Secretary was jarring. I left the number two position in a small, family-owned, heavy-construction firm with one hundred employees at peak periods to take the number two civilian job in the United States Navy, with over one million civilian and military employees.

For two weeks I sat through daily briefings, from eight in the morning till four or five in the afternoon. I spent the lunch hours, between 12 and 2, and the hours between 4 or 5 P.M. and 7 or 7:30 trying to keep up with the paper work.

Fortunately I was surrounded by bright, eager naval and Marine aides and top civilian assistants who kept my office functioning properly. But their brightness made my job even more demanding. If I had been surrounded by mediocre assistants, my own lack of knowledge would have been less obvious.

I felt an additional obligation to do well because I knew I had been forced on McNamara by the President. The weight of the job and my inability to feel that I had it under complete control made me almost despondent at first. If I did poorly, I felt that would be looked upon as an indication that John Kennedy had made some appointments not on the basis of ability but simply out of friendship. I did not realize then that it would take about a year for me to develop the inner confidence necessary to exercise the full responsibilities of the job as I saw it.

During those early weeks in Washington, I was living alone at the Army and Navy Club, a few blocks from the White House. My family was still in Europe.

The President knew I was alone, and had me over for dinner whenever it was convenient.

On Wednesday morning, the first of February, my Marine receptionist, Ginnie Almonte, trying unsuccessfully to remain calm, flashed me and said, "Mr. Fay, the President is on the phone."

"Grand Old Lovable," that unmistakable voice said, "how would you like to see *Spartacus* on Friday night with the President of the United States?"

"Mr. President, I'm with you all the way," I said.

"All right," he continued, "it's playing at the Warner Theatre. Get a couple of good seats for Friday night, but don't

108

let anyone know who they are for. If there is a crowd out there to greet us, I'm going to have your top secret clearance removed." Then he concluded, "Be over here at 7 P.M. for a quick dinner." He hung up.

That afternoon, my driver and friend, Oliver Washington, and I went to the theater and picked up two excellent seats in the center section, about eight or ten rows from the rear. Confident that no one except Washington, as he asked to be addressed, and I knew of the ticket purchase, I was stunned on Thursday morning to get a call from a Secret Service agent.

"Mr. Secretary," he said without any preliminary chitchat, "could you give us the seat row and number for the movie on Friday?"

When I hesitated, he assured me, "It's purely for security reasons." I gave him the information.

After a delicious dinner Friday evening, the President and I went down to the basement, out the south entrance, into the waiting limousine and on to the theater. We arrived just two or three minutes after the picture was scheduled to start. Jack had suggested this slightly tardy arrival to avoid any commotion in the waiting crowd. Nevertheless, the manager and assistant manager were out at the curb, waiting to greet us. I could sense Jack's mild irritation when he saw this slight production developing as he alighted from the limousine. Because I had bought the tickets, I felt a share in the guilt over the existence of the reception committee. Striding rapidly, the President acknowledged the greetings of the manager and assistant manager politely as he hurried into the theater.

The theater was dark but no film was showing. We were directed immediately to our seats.

If any members of the audience noticed us coming in, they gave no indication of recognition. After we were seated, I observed that no one was sitting in any of the rows behind us. At first I didn't understand why. Then I realized that the Secret Service must have instructed the theater management not to sell the seats behind us. From a purely business point of view, I'm sure the manager would have been happy to give the President the entire center section to himself in exchange for the publicity the President provided his theater and the film. I can see the ads: "Come to the Warner Theatre. The man seated next to you might be the President of the United States."

We sat there for a few moments in silent darkness. Finally the crowd started a slow, rhythmical clapping. Obviously the audience was impatient about the delay in starting the film.

Probably overly sensitive to any indication of less than one hundred percent support for the President, I thought at first that the clapping was directed at Jack, and considered it absolutely shameful. I guess all political zealots become so committed to one man or one party that any reflection on him or the party is taken as a personal affront.

After thirty seconds or so, the film started. The crowd cheered. Several days later I found out that the film had actually started a minute or so before we got there, and had been stopped when the President stepped from his car. It was then rewound and shown from the beginning for the President.

While the title and credits were being shown, the President spotted Orville Freeman, his new Secretary of Agriculture, and his wife seated in front of us. Tapping Orville on the shoulder, he asked, "Haven't the leaders of the New Frontier got anything better to do with their time than spend it going to the movies?"

110

Orville replied, with proper respect, "I wanted to be immediately available on a moment's notice if the President wanted me."

They both laughed.

Once the picture was under way, the President was an attentive viewer. His conversation while the film was being shown was limited to an occasional brief remark such as "Look at that guy," or "Amazing acting."

Because of his back injuries, Jack assumed some strange sitting positions while watching films. Sometimes he would put his knee up against the seat in front of him. But I was conscious of his total absorption despite the occasional nervous gestures. Sometimes he tapped his teeth lightly with his index finger, or brushed the hair off his forehead with the full palm of his hand. But always those heavy-lidded eyes were intent on the film.

Spartacus was a long film, broken by a brief intermission. At the break we left our seats immediately and were escorted to the manager's office. I'd been in theater managers' offices before and like all the others I had seen, this one was tucked away back underneath the stairs that led to the balcony. It was so small that you almost met yourself as you came in.

When the manager got the word that the President was coming, he had obviously discussed it thoroughly with his wife and his boss. There was enough liquor in the crowded office to throw a cocktail party for almost everyone in the theater. A large spread of lifeless hors d'oeuvres blanketed a table set up next to the improvised bar. As the intermission of a movie at 9:30 or ten o'clock in the evening doesn't seem the best time to start imbibing, the offerings went untouched. I'm sure the manager felt he had done the right thing, because the Presi-

111

dent was so complimentary about the hospitality. Actually the intermission was a strain for all of us.

After Jack had asked, "Are movies coming back?" and "How long do you think *Spartacus* will run?" there wasn't much else to say. Realizing that at any moment we might all be left standing silently looking at each other, the President attempted to unload the burden of the conversation on me.

"Among Secretary Fay's large circle of friends there has always been a feeling that he had dramatic possibilities," the President said. "Just what kind of roles do you feel he is best adapted to, based on this short period you have had to feel the weight of his personality?"

Not quite sure whether the President was jesting or not, the manager decided it was best to play it straight. He tried to describe the type of role that would be suitable for me, hoping that he could still indicate his own ability to catalogue talent. Jack enjoyed the brief interval while everyone else stood around analyzing my Hollywood potentialities with complete seriousness, however baffled they might have been by the sudden turn of conversation.

He thoroughly enjoyed *Spartacus*. His intimate knowledge of the history of the period and his comments on various leaders of that time made the characters in the film come alive almost as contemporaries.

One of the very few times I discussed the ever-present possibility of an attempt on the President's life came several nights later.

I had had dinner with the President. After seeing a movie in the theater in the basement of the White House, I was say-

112

ing good night when the President said, "I'll walk you to the Army and Navy Club. It's only a few blocks away."

It was a cool, overcast evening, and Lafayette Square seemed almost deserted. We walked out the north entrance of the White House through the gates across Pennsylvania Avenue and into the park of Lafayette Square almost unnoticed. Maybe the image of the new President hadn't yet been firmly established in the minds of the American public, for there were few more striking figures than John Kennedy strolling along hatless in a dark topcoat, swinging a thin cane.

We soon reached the entrance of the Army and Navy Club. Once there, I realized you don't say good night to the President and then let him walk home alone, so we turned around and headed back to the White House again. This time as we entered Lafayette Square I saw a man standing over near the rest rooms looking in our direction. Immediately one of the Secret Service men who had inconspicuously accompanied us on our stroll stepped out ahead. He stood between the stranger and the President and lit a cigarette.

Both Jack and I were very conscious of the whole sequence. I was going to say nothing, because with all his responsibilities I felt some unpleasant topics were much better left undiscussed, but he brought up the subject. Speaking to me in a somewhat hushed voice, he said, "If that fellow over there suddenly pulled a gun, what would you do to safeguard the life of the beloved President?"

As there was no doubt in either his mind or mine that I would take any measure within my power to protect him, I responded in a cavalier manner, "See that freshly turned plot over there? I would dive so hard into its protective soil that

113

there would be room for our beloved President on top of me."

With a laugh he said, "Now and then the true Red Fay does come to the surface."

We walked the rest of the way to the White House mostly in silence. I'm sure both of us were thinking seriously about what we had so lightly discussed. I couldn't dispel the lurking image of an irrational murderer always somewhere poised to strike at the President, any President. If Jack didn't talk of it, it wasn't because he wasn't conscious of the existence of the threat.

He felt all proper precautions were being taken, so on with the job of being the President.

I once asked, "Do you worry about the possibility?"

"I guess there is always the possibility, but that is what the Secret Service is for," he said. Then, after a brief pause: "I guess that is one of the less desirable aspects of the job."

CHAPTER TWELVE

ANITA AND MY four-year old daughter, Sally, were scheduled to reach New York on February 22, 1961.

Shortly before their arrival, the *Constellation,* a carrier, had been badly damaged by fire in the Brooklyn Navy Yard. I asked John Connally, then Secretary of the Navy, if I could take a plane up to New York, inspect the damage and the subsequent repairs to the *Constellation,* and then bring Anita and Sally back with me to Washington for the swearing-in ceremony the next day at the White House. Connally gave me the all-clear.

It was a foggy wet night when I picked up Anita and Sally in New York. "I'm so glad to get off that tremendous big jet and on a nice safe Navy plane," Anita said. In spite of the weather, my naval aide, Bill Golden, said we could fly.

My wife and I were seated in the rear compartment toasting our reunion while Sally was dozing in the forward part of the compartment. Suddenly all the lights went out. At the same time the plane pulled up in a sharp climb, driving us down in our seats.

Having complete confidence in the crew and the equipment, I told Anita, "It's no problem. I'm sure it's just a fuse or something minor. The lights will be on in a minute."

Then I called for Bill Golden, "Bill, what's the problem?"

He went forward and returned in a few minutes with the report.

"They have lost electrical power and are working to get it back."

We continued our champagne party, confident that at any moment the lights would go back on and all would be right with the world. But as time passed and we received no word about progress in restoring power, our conversation became less and less animated. Finally I said, "Bride, I'm going forward to see what exactly is the trouble."

I met Bill Golden coming back from the pilot's cabin.

"They can't get power," he said. "And there is no auxiliary unit. That means we have no radio communications. We can't change the pitch on the props, which were set at full-power pitch for landing, and the wheels can't be brought back up, except manually."

"Well, what are we going to do?"

"All we can do is fly around in a triangular course, which is the indication to ground observers that we are in distress and hope that someone comes up through the soup and leads us to an airfield." Then, to reassure himself as much as me, he added: "I'm sure before long someone will find us and lead us down."

I returned to my seat and told my wife what Bill had said. We sat without saying very much. The added roar of the props at full pitch gave us a feeling that something was about to reach a bursting point.

At least an hour passed, and still there was no change in our pattern. We seemed to be flying aimlessly in a night of gray fog and clouds.

The steward had made up one of the bunks, and we decided to tuck Sally in. But before she would settle into the bunk, she said to me, "Daddy, tell me a scary story."

For years I had been telling all my nieces and nephews scary stories whenever we gathered at Woodside, my childhood home. I tried to tell a scary story, but everything I said paled against what we were actually experiencing.

"Sal," I pleaded, "please go to sleep. Old Dad just can't tell a story now."

An hour and a half had now passed since our loss of power. I spoke to Bill again. "Bill, you're a flier. What do you feel our chances of landing safely are? I don't want to hear something which might make me feel good. I want your true evaluation."

"I figure the chances are one in a hundred that we will get out of this alive," he answered without hesitation.

I hoped the darkness and noise of the engines would conceal my expression of fear.

I felt robbed. My daughter, Kathy, and son, Paul, would grow up and I'd never know where life would take them.

Torn between fear and anger, I asked Bill, "What is our plan? Are we just going to fly around up here till we run out of gas?"

Bill had told me earlier that the props, being set at full pitch, were eating up gas at more than twice the rate they would use if we were flying under normal cruising conditions. The pilot and co-pilot had estimated that our gas supply was sufficient for three hours' flying from the time we lost our electrical power. We had already used up an hour and a half of that valuable time.

"They are going to fly east for an hour, hoping we are over the ocean," Bill said. "They will slowly circle down till we spot the water, then fly west in hopes of picking up the shore and possibly finding someplace to set her down."

Fearing that we might fly too far out over the ocean and not be able to make it back to the coast because of lack of gas, I made my only intervention: "Don't fly east more than a half-hour."

I then came back to Anita and told her everything, including Bill's evaluation of our chances.

Bill advised us that in the event of a crash we should brace our backs against the pilot's compartment. In that way we would not be sent flying through the open area of the cabin itself. We piled mattresses and pillows against the bulkhead.

I unintentionally awakened Sal as I tried to move her from her bed to her mother's arms. When she finally settled down, my wife and I talked quietly about our lives together. Our greatest sadness was at the thought of leaving two young chil-

The Groom greets the Grand Old Usher at the bridal table. Newport, 1953.

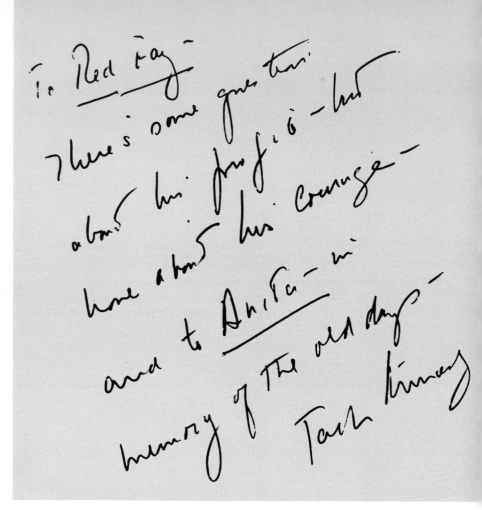

John Kennedy's inscription to Red and Anita Fay on their copy of his book Profiles in Courage: "To Red Fay—There's some question about his profile—but none about his courage—and to Anita—in memory of the old days—Jack Kennedy."

President's inscription on Inaugural invitation to Mrs. Paul B. Fay, Jr who was in Europe at the time her husband was at the Inaugural: "Dea Bride—Where were you? It wasn't the same. I hope to see you soon—John Kennedy."

The Inaugural Committee

requests the honor of your presence

to attend and participate in the Inauguration of

John Fitzgerald Kennedy

as President of the United States of America

and

Lyndon Baines Johnson

as Vice President of the United States of America

on Friday, the twentieth of January

one thousand nine hundred and sixty-one

in the City of Washington

Edward H. Foley
Chairman

A meeting at the Inaugural Parade of four of the warriors of the PT boat days—namely, Ambassador to Australia Bitter Bill Battle, President of the United States Shafty Kennedy, Assistant Secretary of the Treasury Jim Jam Jumping Jim Reed and Under Secretary of the Navy Grand Old Lovable Red Fay—and Vice President of the United States Lyndon Johnson.

President coming home from Sunday Mass aboard the Guardian, *holding spellbound Pat Lawford and Red Fay. Maine, summer, 1962.*

Red Fay, John Kennedy, Ben Smith, Ed Muskie and Jim Reed in 1962.

John being tossed in the air. Camp David, early spring, 1963.

*The Under Secretary of the Navy with friend, feeling very grand.
Palm Beach, Easter, 1963.*

Under Secretary of the Navy sings "Me and My Shadow" for President aboard the yacht of the Secretary of the Navy, the Sequoia, *on occasion of his birthday party, May, 1963.*

Under Secretary of the Navy sings "Hooray for Hollywood" at President's birthday party aboard the Sequoia, May, 1963. *The First Lady is flanked on her left by Bill Walton and Ethel Kennedy and on her right by David Niven and Eunice Shriver.*

Portrait by Sally Fay, age six, acknowledged by President John F. Kennedy: "For my gal Sal—who drew it for her wonderful Dad—JFK."

dren to find a new home and family without the love and support of a father and mother. We also worried about the possibility of Sal being permanently scarred or maimed by the crash if she survived at all. We both said an act of contrition. Then with our hands locked, Sally in her mother's arms, and a rosary entwined in the fingers of the hand of the arm that held her, we sat in silence. Thoughts of the past and what could have been raced through our minds. The minutes passed like eternities.

Knowing that we were fast approaching the time that the pilot estimated we would run out of gas, we listened closely to the roar of the engines. We expected at any minute to hear a series of coughs and chokes and then silence as we plunged into the sea. I reached into my pocket and found a pencil and paper and wrote a note to our two absent children in the darkness:

DARLING PAUL AND KATH:
Your mother, father and Sally are up in this plane without power, so I can't see to write this. It doesn't look too good, but we love you and if we must die now, we know that you will carry on. Your mother is very brave. We have said our prayers and our lives are in the hands of God. All our love.
MOM, SAL, AND DAD

Stuffing the note in my coat pocket, confident that only fire would destroy it, I sat back again with my wife. We both peered through the mist and fog. We couldn't have been more than two or three hundred feet above the water. We finally reached the eastern shore, turned north and flew up the coast. Then suddenly the plane made a sharp turn into a tight circle.

119

I yelled to Bill, "What are we doing?"

"They have spotted a small field and are going to try to land. Brace yourselves for a possible crash because we have no brakes."

Bill ran to the rear of the compartment and buckled himself into a seat as we pressed against the mattresses and pillows which separated us from the bulkhead partitioning off the pilot's cabin. We felt a surge of hope. The plane came out of its tight turn and sank and sank until the lights bordering the airstrip were visible to us through the windows. We bounced lightly on the ground, as if it were a touch-and-go landing. The lights marking the borders of the runway blended as we raced past them. Then, almost before we had comprehended the exhilarating sensation of being saved—crash. Both Anita and I were thrown against the bulkhead. Sally awakened, not crying but startled.

My naval aide jumped to his feet, and there was another crash followed by silence except for a hissing sound. Sighting the water outside, I was convinced that the worst was over, that there would be no explosion, that the plane was a safe haven. My momentary complacency was soon shattered as the pilots came racing out of their compartment warning, "Get out of the plane before we burst into flames."

We tore off the escape hatches. Unable to climb through the exit with Sally, I passed her through to one of the enlisted men who was already out on the wing. Then I noticed Bill Golden making his way with great pain out through the exit.

In a matter of minutes we were all out on the wing. We were in what looked like an estuary about a hundred yards from the quay. Although the plane seemed relatively safe, it was apparent that it was slowly settling and that we would have to get off before too long. People had started to gather on the nearby quay.

Soon a firetruck appeared, but there was no boat. No one seemed to be making a move to come to our assistance. There was no doubt in my mind that my wife and I could swim the hundred yards or so, as cold as the water was, but for Sally that icy swim could have been fatal.

Sally convinced one of the young crew members that Pepito, her stuffed donkey, was alone and crying in the plane. The sailor went back inside and soon emerged, carrying Pepito. I knew she wouldn't leave the plane without him, and carrying the two would have been next to impossible for me.

I yelled, "Please get a boat out here. The plane is sinking."

No one seemed to hear or, if they did, care to answer. Finally after about three or four screams along the same lines, a voice yelled back, "Keep your shirt on, a rowboat is on its way." A few moments later I heard another voice from the beach: "Well, that ought to teach you Navy guys to stay out of the air and stay on the water." We couldn't suppress a laugh.

Before long, two very sorry-looking rowboats, one with one real oar and a coal shovel serving as the other oar, made their way to us. My wife, Sal, one enlisted man and myself stepped into the first boat, and we soon reached shore. The cold, rusty, slime-covered steel ladder up the quay probably hadn't been used for years. With Sally in my arms, one hand for the ladder and one around her, I found those last few steps to the top the longest.

We had crashed in Atlantic City. We rode in a police car, with the red light flashing, to the hospital, even though we

121

felt fine. The doctors discovered that Bill Golden had broken his ankle.

What amazed us almost more than anything else was the alertness of the news media. Photographers greeted us as we came into the hospital. Newspapermen with tape recorders were angling their way past the hospital orderlies to get taped interviews. As soon as we reached the Claridge Hotel, the phone started ringing. A newsman called from California, saying he had picked up the crash on the UPI or AP wire and wanted to know every detail.

Finally I told the hotel phone operator we would accept no more calls till ten the next morning. It was about 2 A.M. by then, so if we received no more calls my wife and Sal would get about eight hours sleep.

At 8 A.M. we were awakened by the phone. Still half asleep, I grabbed it muttering, "Who is it?" On the other end, talking in that bright and cheery tone many people use when they know they have awakened you out of a sound sleep, was another newspaperman. I politely speeded our conversation to an end and then got the operator in the hotel on the phone.

"Young lady, I left a message that we didn't want to be disturbed under any conditions until 10 A.M. Now I repeat, I don't want another call coming into this room till 10 A.M., unless it is the President of the United States."

No sooner had I hung up than the phone rang again. I picked up the receiver to hear the operator say, "Mr. Fay, the President of the United States wants to speak with you."

His first words were, "Are Anita and Sally all right?"

I told him they were.

"Anybody else hurt?"

I replied in the negative, except for Bill Golden's ankle.

Then he said, not attempting to hide his irritation, "And what were they doing on that Navy plane?" Luckily I had asked and gotten permission to make the trip, so I replied, "I cleared with John Connally before I left, and he granted me approval."

Then, recognizing that he had lost hold of an issue which never should have been permitted to arise in the first place, he said, "Fortunately for John, when we lose a half-million-dollar plane, the Navy is just one plane shorter. But the President of the United States is minus one plane plus a hell of a lot of general public support because an Under Secretary of the Navy is flying around in a Navy plane with his wife and child."

There was really no reply for me, so I remained silent.

As if sensing my dilemma, he continued, "Well, I'm pleased no one was seriously hurt or killed. We'll hold your swearing in tomorrow instead of today."

Fortunately, there was no public outcry about Anita and Sal being on the plane, but there were hundreds of stories and photographs in the morning newspapers. The President had read the stories, of course, as he read almost everything in print, and at the swearing-in ceremony he said, "I never knew a fellow who went to such lengths to get publicity for a little ceremony like this."

CHAPTER THIRTEEN

URING HIS FIRST months as President of the
United States, John F. Kennedy had not entirely
lost the feeling that he would still be treated with
some condescension by the Boston Brahmins.

One day he said to me, "Do you know it is impossible for
an Irish Catholic to get into the Somerset Club in Boston? If
I moved back to Boston even after being President, it would
make no difference."

"You're out of your mind," I said. "No club is so bigoted
that it wouldn't ask a President or ex-President to join, regardless of his background, even if he is an Irish Catholic
from Boston."

I got a highly skeptical look from the first Irish Catholic President, and realized that he must on brief occasions imagine he saw signs reading: "Help Wanted—Irish Don't Apply."

He was fascinated and sometimes repelled by the kind of social leader whose life seems to be devoted to rating people and dictating a list of who would and would not be accepted in the so-called social swim.

"Now, what is it that Joan Gardner's got that she can decide who is in and who is out and people accept it?" he asked. (Joan is the daughter-in-law of Arthur Gardner, the former Ambassador to Cuba.)

In August of 1962, Jim Reed, Ed Muskie, Ben Smith, Peter Lawford, Chuck Spalding, the President and I set sail on the Coast Guard sailing vessel, the *Manitou,* from Gene Tunney's John's Island for Dark Harbor, both up in Maine.

On the *Manitou* we all soaked in the sun while the Chief took command of the helm. Whenever the press boat showed up on the horizon or got near enough to take pictures, he ordered all of us to assume the role of members of an alert, well-drilled crew.

"All right now," he would say, with a ring of laughter in his voice, "for God's sake try to look like we have this craft under taut control, and that the leader is giving the image of being the leader."

I still have a picture taken that day that I prize. The President had just said, "My God, Red, pull in that gut." I complied for about sixty seconds, and when I felt I couldn't hold it any longer I pleaded, "Mr. President, image or no image, at the risk of cutting part of our leader out of the picture, I have to

125

let the stomach go back to parade rest." For some reason this produced one of his great smiles.

At Dark Harbor, we stopped briefly at the home of the Watson Blairs, long-time friends of the family. Arrangements had been made earlier for helicopters to pick us up on Josie Blair's back lawn so the *Manitou* could go on to its home port. After an appropriate time, the President indicated that the visit was over. The helicopter was waiting.

There was always something very grand about a Presidential departure, even if he was only taking off from the back lawn of an estate at Dark Harbor, Maine. Not only were the hostess and all her guests there to wave good-bye, but also all the neighbors and all the help. The cooks, the maids, the gardeners, the chauffeurs from the entire neighborhood were out in force. On this day as on many others, one of the cooks could not hold herself back. She broke from the imaginary restraining line and ran up to the President, grasped his hand in both of hers and fervently prayed, "God bless you, Mr. President."

It seemed that the servants were all Irish, came from Boston, and were blessed with the wonderfully generous, uncomplicated personality of the real Irish. The President's response— "Thank you, dear," spoken with warmth and a smile—made the cook realize that he appreciated her bold, natural expression of affection and admiration.

John Kennedy had a very special feeling for the Irish, and especially for the Irishwomen who made their way in life as domestics. It was almost as though he felt any one of them could have been his grandmother or an old maiden aunt. He loved to joke with them. Teddy and Joan had a bright energetic Irish lady in her forties who took care of their children. After his trip to Ireland, John Kennedy couldn't pass her without an exchange in Gaelic. If he thought he was not pronouncing his phrases correctly, he would stop and get a short lesson on proper pronunciation. Then off he would go wishing, *"Céad Míle Fáilte,"* with a sure touch that would challenge the skill of President De Valera.

Few people remained unimpressed by John Kennedy. I do remember one man, an old friend of mine from Stanford who also was a close friend of John Kennedy's brother Joe.

Tom Killefer was a senior when I arrived at Stanford and had gained almost every campus honor. He had been the president of each of his classes, president of the student body during his senior year, Phi Beta Kappa, captain of the baseball team and was selected for a Rhodes Scholarship.

While at Harvard, Tom met young Joe Kennedy. They became close friends in the rivalry to achieve top honors. At Harvard Law School, Tom was elected the president of Lincoln Inn, the best legal fraternity, while Joe had to settle for second place. Both won the Culver Wings during their Navy flight training. Both received the Navy Cross, Joe for volunteering for the dangerous mission that cost him his life.

For some reason, Tom's friendship did not extend to Jack. Instead, there was a certain coolness on Tom's side. What Jack took as an expression of this lack of feeling surfaced in 1944 when Jack was putting together *As We Remember Joe.* Since Tom had been a close friend of Joe's, Jack asked him to write something to be published in the book along with pieces by other friends and notables. Although he repeated the request two or three times, Jack never received a response from Tom.

It wasn't until 1946, when I was back helping campaign for Jack, that Tom's path and mine crossed again. He was then finishing his legal education. Thoughtfully he rang me up at the Bellevue and asked me to join him for lunch.

When I told Jack, he was mildly intrigued. He said, "I'll make a small wager that sometime during the lunch Killefer will tell you that I don't have a chance and never should have run."

I asked, "What gave you that idea?"

"I've heard from other sources that this is his assessment of my chances," Jack said.

There are few more attractive people than Tom Killefer, so our lunch couldn't have been more enjoyable. We talked about various mutual friends, then reached the subject of Jack's campaign.

"I can't help admiring Jack for running for Congress," Tom said, "but from what I can gather he doesn't have much of a chance."

During the Presidential campaign, Tom came out strongly for Nixon. This was not surprising, because he had been appointed the number two man in the Export-Import Bank under the Eisenhower administration. After Nixon was beaten, I'm sure Tom resigned himself to returning to private practice.

When the question of filling Tom's position hit the new President's desk, he asked to see Killefer's record before making a decision.

I would love to know what thoughts raced through Tom's head when he was asked to come down to see the President in his office. He must have thought that the President was just being gracious and wanted to see him personally to wish him well upon accepting his resignation.

"I'm sure when Tom Killefer walked into the office of the President, just about the last person he wanted to say 'Hello, Mr. President' to was Jack Kennedy," the President told me later. "When I told him we wanted him to stay, I'm sure it was even a bigger shock."

Then the President continued: "But he did a good job and top-notch men are hard to find." With a smile, meaning no malice to his former adversary for the Presidency, he added: "Even if Tricky Dick was his man."

While Killefer found it difficult to accept the idea that the kid brother of his own former law society deputy had become President, most other friends of the Kennedys were able to make the adjustment without great difficulty. One partial exception was a summer resident at Hyannis.

One afternoon as the President and I were going off the first tee at the Hyannis Port Club, he asked us if we would like to come over for a drink after our game. They were having a few people in, he said.

"Fine," the President said.

When we reached the house, our host nodded to us both and said, "Jack, come on in. I want you to meet a few of our friends."

After quite a bit of "Jack, I want you to meet . . ." and "Jack, this is . . ." our host probably sensed that his familiarity with the President was making those who were being introduced a little ill at ease. He asked the President, "Should I be calling you 'Jack' like this? We've known each other so long it's hard to call you anything else."

"Whatever makes you feel most at ease . . . it's up to you," the President said, showing no sign of irritation.

"What does Red Fay call you?"

"I think he generally calls me 'Mr. President,'" the President said.

"Maybe I ought to call you 'Mr. President.'"

Now obviously disgusted with the whole discussion, and hoping to bring it to a quick conclusion, the President replied, "Whatever you call me, I'm sure it will be what you think is right."

He turned then to speak to one of the other guests.

When we left, the President said, almost in amazement, "That damn ———— ————, asking me if he should call me 'Jack' or 'Mr. President'! Then he had the guts to imply that he was one of my old pals by asking me what you called me."

I knew that John Kennedy wasn't personally concerned about what anyone called him so long as he rendered due respect to the office of the Presidency. Very, very seldom did I address him as Jack after he became President. It was almost always "Mr. President" or "Chief," an abbreviation of Commander in Chief, as he was to all of us in the Defense Department. There were a few occasions when we were alone and I realized that using the title "Mr. President" or "Chief" might strike him as clumsy. He appreciated the deference I paid the office he held. In return, he would on occasion in a Senatorial tone call me "Paul," just as an indication that he appreciated my respect.

CHAPTER FOURTEEN

A FEW WEEKS AFTER the Inauguration, some of the PT boat warriors arrived in Washington. Johnny Iles, Carlton Byrd, Bill Battle and Al Webb came in with the hope that they would see their old shipmate, "Shafty." They took a suite of rooms at the Sheraton-Carlton, and spent most of the afternoon reminiscing about their World War II experiences. I was planning to join them at 6 P.M., but telephoned in midafternoon to tell them I would not be able to get away from the Pentagon until later.

"Red," Al Webb said, "we would love to give Shafty a call and drop over to see him, but we don't know how to go about it."

131

"Just dial National 8-1414 and ask to speak to the President," I said.

Al laughed at the idea that the President of the United States could be reached in a few seconds through a ten-cent telephone call. I tried to convince him that it was not the price of the call but the name of the man who was calling that would get him through to the Chief.

"When he gets the word about who it is, I'm sure he will come right on, if he is free," I said.

"How do I address him when he comes on the phone?" Al asked. "I can't just say, 'Shafty, this is Nice Al. Can we come over for a couple of hours and swap sea stories?' "

"Say 'Hello, Mr. President,' " I suggested. "Ten chances to one he'll just tell you to come right over."

Al was still skeptical, but by the time we had finished talking he agreed to make the call.

I reached the hotel about 8:30 P.M., and Bill Battle started telling me what had happened.

"Al asked the operator for National 8-1414," Bill said. "Soon the White House operator was on the phone. When Al asked for the President and gave his name, he seemed to be perfectly composed. Even while he was waiting to see if he would really get through to the President, I thought, 'Nice Al has developed a certain sophistication.' "

Johnny Iles broke in. "Red, when Nice Al heard The Man's voice, it was 'choke.' "

Al came to his own defense. "I had just never talked to a President before, and when I heard that voice I didn't know whether to say, 'Shafty, old boy, how are you?' or 'Mr. President, good evening.' "

"So he did neither," Bill Battle said. "Just froze in silence."

"Listen, he knew who it was," Al said, trying to re-establish his image. "All I did was ask for a little help."

"Nice Al passed the conn to Bitter Bill. Then the President asked us all over for a quick drink before dinner and then again after dinner around 9 P.M. to see a movie," added Johnny Iles.

Al said, "When I got on the phone to say good-bye, do you know what he said?"

I replied in the negative.

Al continued, "He said, 'Come over at six. You know my address, don't you?' "

We all roared.

About a quarter of nine the five of us strolled up to the iron gates at 1600 Pennsylvania Avenue. It was obvious from the demeanor of the group that there was a certain lack of confidence in the possibility of our being admitted, even though the four others had been there earlier. Some undoubtedly felt that our proposed visit was going to terminate at this first physical barrier.

As I had an official title, I was elected to negotiate our entrance. The guard called someone on his guard shack phone, and there was a lengthy discussion. The guard came out twice, for more information, and then finally said, "Come right in, gentlemen. The President is expecting you."

We filed through the gates and walked up the half-circle drive which leads to the North Portico. There we were greeted by a butler and a Secret Service man who took our names before we were led to the elevator.

Up we went to the second floor. When the elevator doors opened, we were ushered into the living room that opens on the Truman balcony—the room where I'd taken my lesson on French Impressionist painters.

Within a few minutes, the President walked in. He greeted all of us with his usual friendly manner, but initially the meeting was a little awkward. John Kennedy's transition from Senator to President was a little awe-inspiring to an old friend, even on the second meeting of the day. Everyone was trying to hit just the right note between the old camaraderie and the new respect for the office of the Presidency, and this took a little doing.

We chatted with the President as we walked through the second-floor hall, into the elevator to the basement, and along the long wide hall that led to the movie theater in the East Wing. We took seats beside the President or behind him.

Just before the movie started, there was some talk of having Nice Al sit alone because of the aromatic fish dinner he had just consumed.

"I think if Al just faces toward the screen we'll avoid the impression that this is a fish and game agency film," the President said.

Going to a movie with John Kennedy was always a challenge, and that evening was no different. Because of his back, he changed his position quite often. And you never knew when he was going to become bored with the film and get up and walk out.

We got to see just more than half of the picture before the President had had it. As the President doesn't walk alone, we all exited with him. We chatted for a few more minutes, but it was obvious that the President wanted to go to bed.

Just before we departed, Al said "Mr. President, now that

we are about to leave I can assure you you don't have to worry about strangers getting in here. The way that guard at the gate interrogated us, you better not let your children outside or they might never get back in."

"Here you are worried about getting in here while I'm worried about trying to get out of here," the President said. "If I want to walk across the street, Secret Service men appear from all sides to watch my every move."

As the five of us walked back across Lafayette Square to the Carlton Hotel, we talked about how unbelievable it was that one of our friends was the President of the United States and that we had just left the White House after visiting him.

That night back at the Carlton over a late drink, we sat around reminiscing about great days with John Kennedy, and each of us recalled the first time we ever saw him. . . .

During the first week of November, 1942, I reached the Motor Torpedo Boat Squadron Training Center at Melville, Rhode Island, to become a member of Officers' Class No. 42.

After listening to several indoctrination lectures, with lunch sandwiched in between, we were then led on a mile-and-a-half run around the base by our intrepid P.E. instructor, "Grapes"— so named because of his avowed philosophy: When all other means of defense fail, "go for the grapes." We then found ourselves free for about an hour and a half before dinner, so eight of us organized a game of touch football.

We had been playing fifteen or twenty minutes when a skinny kid came up and asked us if he could join the game. He was wearing a sweater turned inside out, with an "H" sewed on the inside. I assumed that he must be from Hanover

High or whatever the name of the local high school might be. In response to his request I replied, "Get another man to even up the sides and you're in."

He hurried off, and in five minutes or so he was back with another player, who seemed to me because of his size to be the better prospect of the two. After a little negotiating, we unloaded the skinny kid wearing the inside-out sweater on the other team, and our side got the huskier boy.

It took me just a couple of minutes to realize that we had been a little hasty in making our choice. The skinny kid outclassed the heavier one, outran him—and certainly outtalked him.

On the second play after he joined the game, he stopped everything and said we were not following the rules. I protested loudly but the other players, including some of those on my side, agreed with the skinny kid.

Back in the huddle, I remarked, "I'll take that skinny kid from now on."

In the plays that followed, I saw nothing but elbows, shoulders and knees, and acquired a collection of bumps and bruises. The game itself became almost secondary to the battle between the skinny kid and myself at the time of scrimmage— and as always I was definitely not handling the skinny kid. One of my teammates, Don Geyer, a former All-American from Northwestern, pretty well revealed just how inadequate a job I was doing on my self-chosen assignment by asking several times, "Who's got the skinny kid?"

The next morning, I reported to the dock for my first instructions in boat handling. I recognized the instructor immediately: it was the skinny kid, no longer wearing his Harvard sweater with the "H" on the inside. There, in the uniform of a lieutenant, junior grade, was John F. Kennedy.

Later that morning I had my first face-to-face meeting with John Kennedy as an officer. I had been assigned to his command, an older boat, the 77-footer design, for the boat-handling drill, but decided to jump aboard one of the newer 80-footers instead. This caused considerable confusion, and delayed Lieutenant Kennedy, his crew and his group of students ten or fifteen minutes.

When I returned to the base, I was ordered to report to the Lieutenant's Quonset hut immediately. If everybody behaved as irresponsibly as I had, he told me, the Japanese could be marching through Times Square within a few weeks. He was thinking of recommending that I be dropped from Motor Torpedo Boat training because of my failure to follow orders. I practically got down on my knees to ask for a second chance, and he finally relented.

That day I felt no strong desire to cross paths with young Lieutenant Kennedy again. But a few months later in the South Pacific we became friends.

In August, 1943, while we were getting ready to move the last three boats in our squadron up to the island of Rendova, we received word that PT 109 had been rammed by a Japanese destroyer. According to the report, the PT 109 had exploded and had been totally consumed by fire.

I knew Lieutenant John Kennedy was in command of the PT 109, but at the time I felt even more bitter about the loss of

137

George "Barney" Ross. Barney, whom I had also met at Melville, was then my closest friend in the service, and I mentioned his name first when I wrote to my younger sister, Sally:

George Ross lost his life for a cause he believed in stronger than any one of us, because he was an idealist in the purest sense. Jack Kennedy, the Ambassador's son, was on the same boat and also lost his life. The man that said the cream of a nation is lost in war can never be accused of making an overstatement of a very cruel fact.

My grief was compounded by the realization that Barney had not been ordered to go out on that mission, but had merely gone along for the ride. At that time, I did not know Jack Kennedy well enough to feel the same kind of deep personal loss. I did feel that an unusually intelligent and attractive man with a great deal to live for had been deprived of his chance in life.

When I heard that no bodies had been recovered and no sign of the wreckage found, I began to wonder about just what had happened to the PT 109. I thought at least a life jacket or a bit of wooden hull should have been found floating in the area where the ship went down.

Another boat had been operating with the PT 109 that night, and one day while I was walking along the wharf at Tulagi I ran into the skipper of that other boat.

"Did you see the explosion?" I asked him.

"Yes," he said.

"Did you go over to the spot to look for survivors?"

"Yes," he said.

"You mean there were no bodies, no sign of debris, nothing at all? Everything had disappeared?"

"Yes," he said.

"You can't tell me there wasn't some trace of the boat," I said. "In my book you are a liar. You never went back to the scene of the explosion."

The officer was senior to me in rank, but he did not challenge me. He simply walked away, mumbling, "I won't take that from you, Fay."

But others continued the search, and through their persistence and the ingenuity of Jack Kennedy, the survivors of the PT 109 were rescued a few days later.

By that time, we had received orders to take our PT boat on to Rendova. On our way, we passed the boat carrying Jack Kennedy, Barney Ross and the other survivors. Big Barney waved to us as we passed, as if he were out on a Sunday cruise on San Francisco Bay.

A few months later, an incident involving our PT boat led to my friendship with John F. Kennedy.

We were returing from Bougainville with a broken V-drive on our center engine, and were escorting an LCT and an LCI. It was dusk and I was arguing with a Marine correspondent about football when one of the lookouts turned to me and said, "Mr. Fay, there are some planes coming in on our port side."

I took a quick look and said, "Just SBD's, don't worry," and went back to my discussion. I couldn't have talked more than another ten seconds before I realized that I had done something wrong in assuming the planes were U.S. Navy dive bombers.

I looked up again at the onrushing planes and screamed, "Japs!"

The gunner was way ahead of me. He had his twin fifties cocked and trained, ready to fire as soon as the planes came within range.

The Japanese heading toward us were flying not more than ten or fifteen feet above the water. One plane, aiming directly at our bow, banked to avoid our bridge. It clipped its wings on the gunwale, and crashed into the sea about one hundred yards from us.

Having made their torpedo run, the Japanese pilots circled back to bring us under machine-gun fire again. This was a mistake. The combined fire power of the PT boat, the LCT and the LCI was too much for them. We saw one Japanese pilot fighting to climb out of the cockpit just after his plane burst into flame, but the canopy wouldn't open. He crashed about two hundred feet in front of us. Off to our right we could see two more planes falling in flames, brought down by the gunners on the LCI under the direction of their standout gunnery officer, Peter Kirill.

By now darkness had closed in. Ted Berlin, our skipper, told me to go below to see if there was any damage. I grabbed a flashlight and walked forward into the crew's quarters. Just after I reached there, I heard someone topside scream, "Submarines!"

"My God," I thought, "they're throwing the entire Japanese fleet at us!"

Then I realized what had happened. The Japanese plane that crashed over our bow had dropped its torpedo so low that the torpedo had skipped along the surface of the water like a rock. It had not fired, but had torn a great gaping hole in our boat just above the water line. My light, flashing through that hole, had led all hands topside to imagine attacking submarines.

We made it down to Tulagi for repairs without any further evening contact. Jack Kennedy was there, resting to regain his health.

I'm sure my friendship with Jack Kennedy grew partly because we were both from large, Irish Catholic families. I admired him tremendously, and he and I appreciated the same type of people.

During the weeks at Tulagi, a group of us would meet up at Jack's tent before dinner three or four times a week. His tent was set up in the back of the base, almost in the jungle. There he would conduct informal seminars, which resembled radio discussion shows. We talked about foreign policy, politics, military strategy, military leadership, education and—infrequently, because we tried to keep them out of the discussions —girls. Jack always emphasized that we had no right to complain about political decisions unless we exercised some leadership in local or national politics.

There was no question in my mind or the minds of Barney Ross, Jim Reed and Byron White that Jack Kennedy was an exceptional man. Barney and I made book in 1943 that someday Jack Kennedy would be President of the United States. We set the odds at ten thousand to one, because he was still out in the war zone, his health was poor, he was young and unforeseen circumstances could make it impossible for him to reach the White House. Barney and I, with considerable conceit, placed the odds on ourselves as Presidential possibilities at somewhere between one million and two million to one, and we could have gotten all the takers we wanted at those odds. But Jack Kennedy's greatness was so apparent to me that I did something very unusual for a man. I saved every letter or note that he ever sent me, beginning during the war years.

Jack's strong sense of responsibility could not conceal his love of living and his genuine enjoyment of a joke. One lazy day still out in the Pacific at Tulagi, Ed McLaughlin our disbursing offier, was the target. Ed, a tall slender Irishman from Boston who eventually became the Lieutenant Governor of Massachusetts, had dark red hair and a temper to match. Nine months earlier he had lost one hundred dollars during one pay period, even though he always stood with a .45 pistol strapped to his hip watching each bill as it was counted out. The hundred-dollar loss was discovered when he was checking his cash at the conclusion of his pay period, and everyone from the skipper down to the lowest apprentice seaman was accused of the robbery. For some reason I always felt Ed thought I had taken the hundred dollars or knew who had taken it.

I had told Jack Kennedy of the incident, so on this relatively peaceful day, just before lunch, Jack said, "Ed McLaughlin is going to have a pay day today. Why don't we see if he is up to the occasion?"

We knew that Ed was then in the next tent, in the middle of a poker game. As part of the plan worked out with Jack, Barney and I slipped out of our tent and walked over to the place where the public address system was located. We slipped into the little shack, switched on all speaker outlets, and then announced: "Attention all hands, attention all hands. This is your disbursing officer. Today is pay day. Those who need cash

142

badly please come early, because we're not sure where all the money is."

We snapped off the equipment and ran over to hide behind a tent about ten yards away. Even as we ran we could hear the door slam as Ed came roaring out of his tent, cursing and swearing at everyone in sight. Although he didn't catch us, when Barney and I came over for our pay that afternoon we were greeted by a glowering paymaster. "So help me, Ross and Fay, I know it was you. I'll get you two bastards someday. This place has been a madhouse since one o'clock with everyone yelling, 'Don't run out of money till I get mine.'"

When the first shipment of draftee sailors reached Tulagi from the States, Jack was still recuperating from the collision. An officer was needed to indoctrinate the new group, and Jack volunteered. When the Chief notified Lieutenant Kennedy that the men were lined up down by the flagpole, I walked down with him. Dressed in his worn and faded khaki, his hair pushing out from beneath his salty, weathered cap, thin and gaunt, he stepped before that group.

Jack started to talk in a relatively quiet tone, which made it difficult for the sailors in the rear to hear. They started to edge forward, and before long any semblance of rank was gone. Those on the outer edges of the crowd were jumping up and down, shouting, "What did you say Lieutenant?" Finally he restored order.

To conclude his talk, Jack said to the men, "If there is ever anything I can do for you, please let me know." Many years later when he was a Senator and we were reminiscing about the Pacific, he remarked, "If ever there was a statement I regretted making it was the one I made that day to those sailors about 'if there is ever anything I can do for you. . . .' They are still

143

coming in saying, 'Senator, remember that day when you said
. . .' I don't even wait for them to finish the statement any
more!"

Soon after Jack returned to the States, he wrote me from the
New England Baptist Hospital in Boston:

(Written on my back so writing will be one by one)
DEAR RED:

Glad to hear from you and get the news both late and strate.
I regret that I did not get a chance to look over the establishment
of the Fay Construction Company—sell a few bonds—and talk
with the impresario himself but due to what is known in train
circles as "an extremely close connection," I had time for only
a short pilgrimage up Nob Hill on my knees to light a candle—
and then I executed Tare 90° & headed southward where I
spent my next four days . . . in lower California. I did have
the pleasure of communicating with the young Fay girl & sending her the pictures to be forwarded to the great industrialist. I
also put in a few plugs for you which I hope they will take
seriously but which I trust you won't—as we both know how
consistently you've been dropping the ball out there. The picture of Ross Park—somewhere in the Solomons—is a moving
one—wherever that mighty man moves he leaves his mark. Time
will never erase from my mind the picture of that tall gaunt
figure stopping me at a touch ball game at Melville. Hey, Bub,
where did you get that sweater with the H, huh? When he
thought he was going to die one night on the island, he con-
fessed to me he thought that I was an enlisted man and had
stolen it—and it took quite a bit of juice power for me to keep
from pushing his head under water for a period.

Haven't been down to Melville as yet—but did get to the base
at Miami, where it looks like no strain. The squadrons are piling
up there—they are turning them out faster than they can get

144

them out there. I was extremely glad to hear that the relief situation was finally getting worked out and that you and Ted had your prospects for getting out this spring.

Tell Moriarity I talked with his folks and they sounded fine. Spent the weekend up in Boston where I gave an exhibition of talking where I should have been listening.

The States is just about what you would think. Everyone very optimistic and it's very true that "hell hath no fury like a civilian"—and when I read the papers I think the war will be over tomorrow—but I know it won't. You don't have any chance to tell any war stories as everyone is too busy telling you one. . . . The bull some guys are handing out here is unbelievable. The favorite question they ask you is "How many destroyers did you get?" If you didn't get at least five, which they think makes you an ace and is par for the course, there is no sense coming home. There is no sense in handing out any bull though—it's *nice* to be home—and I sincerely hope to see you boys soon back here or back here soon (which is better English? Ever since I went to Stanford I've had trouble with my English).

I'm in the hospital for another couple of weeks on my back—& then down to report at Melville—& then in a month or so later I'm afraid I'm going to have to have an operation on it—but perhaps it will all work out.

Best to Ted & Barney and all the boys. Tell Barney that there has been a slight case of mislaying of addresses re B. T. Sweetie, but when I get out of here—I will make my Pilgrimage to the shrine. I talked with Jude the Obscure—the beloved of James Reed—she sounded extremely nice. Will call Burkett. Drop me a line.

Best,
JACK

("The impresario" and "the great industrialist" are friendly references to my father. "That mighty man" and "tall gaunt figure" refer to the great George "Barney" Ross. Moriarity, an Irishman from Boston, was the cook on Ted Berlin's and my boat. Ted was skipper until I took over just before we moved over to New Guinea. "Jude the Obscure" is a reference to Jewel Reed, then Jim Reed's wife. Burkett refers to a beautiful Stanford coed, Nancy Burkett, now Mrs. Robert Morse, whom we both took out back before and during the war.)

In February, 1944, I had another letter from him, written from the Castle Hot Springs Hotel, in Castle Hot Springs, Arizona:

DEAR RED:

I'm sorry I haven't come through with a report on how the Irishman is doing. Frankly, Red, it's a bit slow. Either they haven't read the August issue of the *Reader's Digest* or something, for every time I introduce Kula Gulf into the circle (in itself no mean feat), the conversation just seems to pick itself up and walk into a corner and die. In all fairness to myself I've got to admit it's a tough audience—former Presidents of the local Kiwanis, who have put in their three score and ten and are half way round again. When you fire a fast one at them— that's high and just hitting the corner of the plate, they make no attempt to go for it; they just *know* that they have one that is going to knock you right off that easy chair. I don't mean that in a derogatory sense—but you wouldn't get a ripple out here with the Sarge—unless the tousle-headed lieutenant saved you as he has so often in the past. I'm not knocking the Sarge— it's just that Castle Hot Springs is where self-panickers come to die.

Nevertheless, the facilities are excellent—good swimming pool and hot baths, and a rubber in charge who is a poor man's Sergeant Casey—being an ex-marine and now a rubber and combining the loquacious characteristics of both professions.

146

The food is just fair—but you can have all you want for thirty bucks a day. If I stay here very long, I'm going to end up my life scratching a beggar's ————. What are your plans? . . . Are you coming out here? I hope so because I'd like to get started socially in Burlingham—but I suppose we would hang around the fire-house all the time waiting for your old man to put out a fire. . . .

I don't believe I told you about my meeting with Robert Kelley—the Manilla Gorilla. When he asked me where I was going I told him Arizona and I took the better part of a morning to explain the difference between the U.S.S. *Arizona* (and) Arisona USA.

The news about the post-war drive of Red Fay's straight-men was good news but while I agree that the Coot Kid and the Big George and the Rod and Shafty boy etc. will all end up as buddies, what do you think about Mrs. Coot Kid and Mrs. Rod and Mrs. Barney Boy and Mrs. K. (money on both sides)? Is there any possibility that they will take a dim view of the old Redhead? Please answer this question in your next.

Best,

SHAFTY

P.S. Throughout this letter I have had the feeling that I've written it before—perhaps to you. If so, just shake it off & remember that my gag writer is now writing editorials for *Life*.

("Sarge" is Sergeant Tom Casey, one the great figures of the Stanford–Palo Alto area. "Burlingham" is a reference to Burlingame, which I had described as the social apex of the San Francisco Bay area. The reference to my father and putting out fires is a result of his being also the Fire Commissioner in Woodside. Robert Kelley is the Kelley of PT boat fame, who along with John Bulkeley brought General MacArthur out of the Philippines. "Coot Kid" is Quentin "Cootie" Thompson, former Stanford baseball captain—great pitcher—now an insurance executive. "Big George" and "Barney Boy" is Barney Ross. "Rod" is John C. Warnecke, former Stanford All-American tackle in the Rose Bowl, now a distinguished architect and the architect for the President's grave.)

By November, 1944, he was back in Massachusetts and wrote to me from the U.S. Naval Hospital in Chelsea:

DEAR RED:

Needless to say, the old eyes filled a bit when I got your dispatch from your beach-head in Hollywood. I appreciated your offer to share your fox-hole and I have delayed answering until I have a definite idea of what's going to be done. Unfortunately or fortunately, depending on how you look at it, and I won't ask for a statement—some time in the next month I'm going to be paying full price at the local Loew's. I will no longer [be] getting the forty-per-cent off for servicemen—for the simple reason that I'm going to be in mufti. This I learned yesterday—as they have given up on fixing me up O.K. From here I'm going to go home for Christmas, then go to Arizona for about a year, and try to get back in shape again.

In any case, I'll be in Palm Beach fairly soon—so you'll have to come up for a few weekends as the facilities are ample for even a guy who throws his weight around like you. Pappy is going down with Commissioner Timilley the 29th of November. Anyway, I hope for a guest-star spot from you for Christmas. At the Kennedies' own Christmas, the wassail flows like molasses, but the chow is excellent.

Drop me a line up here if you get the chance, as I am based here now.

Best,
JACK

CHAPTER FIFTEEN

ACK HAD DECIDED to assemble and edit a book about his brother, Joe, and to present it to his parents at Christmas, 1944. He had devoted hundreds of hours to the job of collecting material from those who had known Joe, and had arranged to have the book printed at a cost of around five thousand dollars.

Unfortunately, the printer did not have *As We Remember Joe* ready by Christmas Day. After all his work, Jack had no presents ready for his mother and father or family on December 25, 1944.

Mrs. Kennedy had very generously asked me to spend Christmas Day with Jack and the family. Since my own family was three thousand miles away, I accepted the invitation eagerly and then went down to the local drugstore on Christmas Eve to pick up some small gifts for the Kennedys. I did not have a lot of cash with me, and I must have spent about ten dollars altogether for the presents.

Some girl had lost the tail of her silver fox wrap wrestling with Jack Day, a fellow officer at the Hollywood Beach Hotel officers' school, in the back of my Model T Ford. I found it and put it in a box with a bow on it. That became my Christmas present for Mrs. Kennedy. All my gifts were trinkets with about as much substance as the fox tail.

The evening before Christmas we all decorated the tree. Jack kept joking with me and the others, trying to keep his father's and mother's minds off Joe. This was the first Christmas since Joe's death.

When Christmas day rolled around, there I was with ten or fifteen trifles for the Kennedys. With the fox tail I included a note: "Merry Christmas, Mrs. Kennedy. There is a strong feeling that fox tails will be the rage this season. Affectionately, Red Fay."

Jack watched the reception of my presents with disbelief. Even though no one of them was worth more than a dollar or two, the mere number of them made his lack of gifts for the family more noticeable.

After all the packages had been opened, Mrs. Kennedy couldn't hide her disappointment. She took Jack down the hall and said: "Red Fay isn't even a member of the family, but he was thoughtful enough to give all those nice presents to the family, and here it's your own family and you don't have the thoughtfulness to remember any of us at Christmas."

Jack told me later that he started to explain, but then figured his was a lost cause. "Here I am spending five thousand dollars, working my head off to give something that really means something to my dad and mother, and what happens? You come down here with ten dollars' worth of drugstore supplies, the tail of somebody's silver fox wrap, and you're the star of the day. What am I, an inconsiderate, selfish adult who doesn't love his family? Thanks, Pal."

During that visit to Florida, Jack and I sometimes came in after a game of golf and enjoyed a few beers followed by a bourbon or two. For some reason, Joseph Kennedy had developed a strong feeling about anyone in the family or even friends of the family taking more than a single drink before dinner.

If Jack had been alone, I think he would have settled quickly enough for a cold beer or one before-dinner drink. But he relished the intrigue involved in getting drinks without being detected by the boss. Dave, the chauffeur-butler, would slip these into Jack's room at the end of the south wing while we were dressing for dinner.

Then we would go join the rest of the family, and there we would be served the single cocktail Joseph Kennedy considered sufficient. I would finish it in the few minutes allotted, and since I had had the head start in Jack's room, all was right with the world. But invariably Jack would say to his father, as though he were looking after a friend who suffered from a deep and irrational craving for booze, "Dad, is it all right if Red has another drink before dinner?"

No matter how firmly I tried to indicate that I could cheerfully go on to the table without any further fortification, the damage was done. Mr. Kennedy would give me a look that indicated no sympathy at all for my unfortunate weakness, and say brusquely: "We're going in to dinner right now."

Obviously relishing the entire scene, Jack would pass me on the way in to dinner and say, "I'll try to explain to Dad that you have yourself in check."

During those months just after his discharge from the Navy, I'm convinced Jack saw his future as a writer—perhaps as a newspaper columnist commenting chiefly on politics. But gradually his ambitions changed in the months after his brother Joe's death.

He knew that his father now saw him as the heir to the political traditions of the family. "I can feel Pappy's eyes on the back of my neck," he once said to me during this period.

Early in 1945, when I was stationed at Hollywood Beach, Florida, and came up almost every weekend to visit Jack, he first indicated to me that he had reached his decision.

"Red," he said one day, with no special enthusiasm, "when the war is over and you are out there in sunny California giving them a good solid five and a half inches for a six-inch pavement, I'll be back here with Dad trying to parlay a lost PT boat and a bad back into a political advantage. I tell you, Dad is ready right now and can't understand why Johnny boy isn't 'all engines ahead full.' "

Although at that time Jack seemed indifferent to the whole idea of a political career, you sensed his movement in that direction. I wasn't surprised early in 1946 when he made the firm decision to run for Congress—and when he asked me to come East to campaign for him, I came.

When I walked into the Bellevue Hotel in Boston, all ready to go to work for Jack, I happened to meet him as he was

152

coming down in the elevator. He was with two or three other people, on his way to some campaign meeting.

"Red," he said, "it's good to see you. I'm going to a couple of meetings. Why don't you go up to the room, and I'll see you when we get back." He handed me the key to the room, and off he went.

And that was it.

I thought, "God, is the sort of reception I get, after coming three thousand miles?" I was ready to catch the next plane back to California, but I decided to wait and tell Jack my reasons first. "Obviously you don't need me," I was going to say. "What a wild-goose chase this was."

I went up to his room to wait.

I had nothing to do for about two hours but stare at the four walls. After the first few boring minutes, I succumbed to a very unattractive weakness and started going through Jack's mail. The desk drawers were filled with unpaid bills, unanswered invitations, letters that hadn't even been opened.

I made a list of all the bills, wrote out checks to pay them, addressed the envelopes, stamped them, and made a list of all the speaking invitations.

When Jack returned, I said, "Well, I don't know how much longer I'm going to be here. Anyway, before I leave at least you can sign these checks, so we can get these people paid."

Recognizing my irritation, he knew exactly how to handle me. "God, no wonder there has been no organization around here," he said. "Nobody around here was big enough to recognize the candidate's real problems and do something to correct them. Red, you're staying right here to get this campaign running on a businesslike basis."

Flattery will get you everywhere, at least with me. All my

irritation vanished. I was suddenly right in the middle of John Kennedy's first political venture.

I became a kind of coordinator and a companion for the candidate. People were breaking down the doors to help him, so it was just a matter of organizing them to make real use of their abilities. Before long we had replaced total chaos with organized confusion.

On my second day in Boston, the candidate was scheduled to attend a meeting at the Parker House in the late morning. Well in advance of the time set, we started toward the hotel. We couldn't go ten steps without someone stopping to shake Jack's hand or wish him encouragement. We stopped for a moment to chat with a very distinguished-looking older gentleman. During the brief meeting, he put a roll of bills into Jack's handkerchief pocket with the simple statement, "Jack, here is a contribution for your campaign. You have my every good wish."

Jack thanked him, and after shaking hands we parted.

That evening as we were getting ready to go to bed, I inquired, "Jack, how much did that gentleman give you this morning in the way of a campaign contribution?"

Obviously having forgotten the incident, he replied, "My God, do you know I never even looked." He walked over to the closet, reached into the outside coat pocket of his suit and pulled out ten new one-hundred-dollar bills.

I don't remember having even seen ten one-hundred-dollar bills together outside of a bank. I'm sure this was not the case with Jack, but he was as much overwhelmed as I was. With a look of amazement he said, "And all he said was, 'Here is a contribution for your campaign.' Wait until I tell Dad. It will make him awfully pleased. Mr. ———— is a friend of his. That is support."

One day Jack's grandfather, "Honey Fitz" Fitzgerald, who had once been Mayor of Boston, took Jack down to City Hall. Honey Fitz said he would introduce Jack to the city workers, and tell them that his grandson was running for Congress and needed their support.

No sooner had we reached City Hall than Honey Fitz started shouting greetings to old friends. Soon his arms were waving, and the next thing you knew he was singing "Sweet Adeline," and all the city workers in the huge room were singing it with him.

When he finally stopped singing and waving, he said, "Come on, Jack, Let's go."

Glancing at me with a look that seemed to ask, "Did you expect anything else?" Jack turned to Honey Fitz and said, "Gramp, notwithstanding the impression to the contrary, it is your grandson who is running for office, not the beloved former Mayor. Do you think we could try and get that message over before we leave?"

Not at all disturbed, Honey Fitz nodded.

"Oh, yes, ladies and gentlemen, I want to introduce my grandson. . . ."

In spite of the excitement and the companionship of the candidate, I was champing to get back to San Francisco and the Bride (as she was known by all my friends during our engagement). On top of that the Battler had given me the ultimatum, "Get back by one May or there won't be any job for you." And there had been a few rumbles among the local pols, best expressed by Patsy Mulkern, a local ward-heeler.

"Why the hell do we have to take orders from a God-damn redhead from San Francisco? Him telling me to wait outside, the candidate was busy. What the hell does a guy from Frisco know about Boston politics."

With all this the candidate tried to persuade me to stay, if for nothing more than companionship. Since he had met Anita in San Francisco at the time of the formation of the UN in 1945, about six or eight months before I did, he attempted to play on my imagination. Seeing me poring over the last letter I'd received from her, which had me smarting because she spent almost the entire letter telling me about going out with Frank McGinnis and calling him "Red" all night, the candidate passed me a bundle.

"By the way, Red," he said, "did Anita ever tell you about that Air Force flier? The good-looking one that—" He broke off in the middle of the sentence with a guilty look, as if he had said something which shouldn't have been told. Although I knew just what was happening, I bit right in. Visions of some dashing, irresistible flier making mad love to my darling crept into my mind. Obviously my face had betrayed my thoughts, because Jack said with a tone of solace, "I'm sure it was just a passing fancy for both and meant nothing."

One day word came that Bobby Kennedy had gotten leave from the Navy and was coming up to help Jack in the campaign for the weekend. I'd met Bobby at Palm Beach several years earlier, and remembered him only as a small, very quiet boy.

"It's damn nice of Bobby wanting to help," Jack told me, "but I can't see that sober, silent face breathing new vigor into

156

the ranks. The best plan is to make it known to the press. One picture of the two brothers together will show that we're all in this for Jack. Then you take Bobby out to movies or whatever you two want to do."

"Fine," I said. I decided I would take Bobby to a movie house in Boston that also featured vaudeville.

Young Bobby arrived. I knew he was there only because I could see him. Words came out of his mouth as if each one spoken depleted an already severely limited supply.

When I suggested the movie and vaudeville, his reply was a quiet, expressionless "All right." Off we went, with me trying my best to make conversation. Bobby's total contribution was an occasional "yes" or "'no."

Once we reached the theater, the movie gave me a chance to break off the struggle to keep communication alive. Then the vaudeville began. After several tumbling and juggling acts, a comedian came on stage. He was hilarious. Certain that I had made a good choice for a place to entertain my ward for the evening, I looked over to make sure he was enjoying this as much as I was. From his expression, he might have been paying his last respects to his closest friend.

I turned back toward the stage, with my enthusiasm markedly reduced. When three more uproarious jokes failed to raise a chuckle from my partner for the evening, I suddenly found all my own pleasure draining away. About ten minutes of this was all I could handle.

"Shall we go?" I asked Bobby.

Without hesitation, he got up and the two of us filed out in absolute silence.

As we came out of the theater that day, I would have cheerfully taken bets against the possibility that I would ever volunteer to spend an hour with Bobby Kennedy again. But I would have lost. In the years since, I've spent hours, evenings, weekends and entire vacations with him—and enjoyed them all.

During the mid-1940's, I also spent some time with Joseph Kennedy, and I particularly remember two revealing moments with him on golf courses in Massachusetts and Florida. One day I joined him for a game on the Cape, and someone waved to him from the other green and shouted, "Hello, Joe, how are you?"

Mr. Kennedy looked up and returned the wave. Then he turned back toward me and said with a touch of humor, "You know, Red, that fellow thinks I'm smiling at him."

When in the sun and squinting, Joe Kennedy also exposed his teeth and this gave the impression that he was smiling.

A few months later, during another game of golf at Palm Beach, we were held up on every one of the first four holes by the twosome in front of us. Mr. Kennedy was angered by the third delay, and by the fourth tie-up he was fuming. Finally, he shouted ahead, "Bill, if you want us to come through, just let us know."

Bill nodded, indicating that he would let us know.

"Before the depression, that guy used to be worth 35 or 40 million dollars," Joe Kennedy said. "Now he would be lucky if he could scrape together two or three millions, and he's still acting like he had it."

"The poor fellow," I said, tongue in cheek. "How does he manage?"

But back to the candidate himself. Because of all the demands on his time, Jack had forgotten to file his nomination papers. On the final filing date, one of his campaign workers asked casually, "Jack, when did you file your nomination papers?"

A look of shock crossed the candidate's face.

"My God," he muttered, "they haven't been filed."

It was about 6:30 and the office where the papers had to be filed had been closed since 5 P.M. A series of frantic phone calls was made. Then, very quietly, the candidate and some loyal public retainers went down, opened up the proper office and filed the papers.

Another couple of hours, and all of the thousands of hours of work by the candidate and his supporters would have been completely wasted.

Jack was easily re-elected to Congress in 1948 and 1950. In November, 1950, he wrote me: "The campaign came through all right. I am all set for the big run in 1952. I hope you will be able to get away for a few days. I need you for the campaign picture: 'Famous Stanford Great Advises Navy Friend.' "

CHAPTER SIXTEEN

ONE DAY IN July, 1953, Jack wrote me:

I gave everything a good deal of thought—so am getting married this fall. This means the end of a promising political career as it has been based up to now almost completely on the old sex appeal. I hope you and the bride will be able to come—the date is Sept. 12th—as I need you to come down the aisle with me. Your special project is the bride's mother—one fine girl—but who has a tendency to think I am not good enough for her daughter.

As I am both too young and too old for all this—will need several long talks on how to conduct yourself during the 1st 6 months—based on your actual real life experience.

Let me know the general reaction to this in the Bay area.

Your buddy,

JACK

Anita and I accepted.

Ten days before the wedding, about 350 of Jack's friends, including his campaign chairmen from all parts of Massachusetts, gathered at the Parker House in Boston to host a bachelor dinner for the junior Senator from Massachusetts.

Bob Kennedy and I had been on a cruise along the coast of Maine with our wives, Teddy Kennedy, and his sister Jean, and Dave Hackett. We were scheduled to give short speeches at the dinner so we spent about an hour and a half during our cab ride to the Parker House preparing our offerings.

When the time came for Bob to get up before that crowd to make his speech, he was ashen white. His hands quivered and his voice quaked. He got through his speech on pure guts, not missing a line. When he finished you could almost feel the audience's relief.

The next time I heard Bob deliver a speech was in 1960, in San Francisco shortly after the convention. It was impossible to believe it was the same man. He had complete command of his subject and spoke with ease, wit and persuasion.

After the bachelor dinner, Jack offered to drop some of the guests off at their homes. One of the men he invited to join us worked in a factory during the day and did odd jobs in the evening to make ends meet. Another was running a laundry, and the third was a bus driver.

I was amazed at Jack's understanding of how tough it was for them to eke out a living. His obvious admiration for them—for the fact that they were willing to moonlight to support their families—gave them all an added sense of achievement. But even more important to them was the sincere deep interest that he had in them as individuals.

After they had gotten out and we drove on to Newport, I thought back to the days just after World War II when I had trouble getting Jack to repay twenty bucks I had loaned him.

I don't know exactly what brought about the change, but in six or seven years Jack had learned what money meant to men who were not the sons of Joseph P. Kennedy. He had never been callous, but in earlier years he just did not think about money—his own or anyone else's. Now he knew how important a matter it was to most of the people in the world.

When we reached Newport late that evening after the long drive from Boston, I had my first meeting with Jacqueline Bouvier. Shortly after Jack and I reached the house, she came down in a bathrobe and slippers. Her wide-eyed beauty, her grace and quiet ease of manner caused me to show her unusual deference for someone in her early twenties. When she spoke I was fascinated by her voice, so soft and clear.

With all her sophistication, she couldn't conceal her love for Jack. Because I was there, Jack was slightly self-conscious. After giving her a relatively quick kiss and embrace, he turned, partly breaking the embrace and said, "Jackie, this is Red Fay."

We went into the kitchen for a glass of milk and freshly baked chocolate-covered pan cake. While we ate and talked, Jacqueline would reach for Jack's arm or hand, and speak with great delight of their coming marriage. She laughed. She almost sang. She did all the things a young, beautiful girl does when she is in love and the man she loves is with her.

The Senator, who was then thirty-six, tried to appear casual about all the affection coming his way, but obviously was thoroughly enjoying every second. I soon found an excuse to go up to my room and leave them alone for a few minutes.

162

Moments later Jack came upstairs to the third floor, where we were to stay. Mildly curious about his old friend's opinion, he asked, "Well, what do you think of Jackie?"

"God, she's a fantastic-looking woman," I said. Then I added, "If you ever get a little hard of hearing, you're going to have a little trouble picking up all the transmissions."

Jack threw back his head and roared. He was obviously so smitten that any remark, any observation, even if it could be interpreted as slightly critical, was enjoyable because it was about Jacqueline.

But a marriage between a beautiful, enamored young lady and a worldly public figure in his mid-thirties is not as simple a matter as the union of a teen-age boy with the girl next door.

When Jack and Jacqueline came to the West Coast on their honeymoon, the pressures of public life—not to mention those of an old shipmate and his wife—too often intruded on the kind of honeymoon any young bride anticipates. For example, on Jack's and Jacqueline's last day on the West Coast, Jack and I went to a pro football game while his bride of several weeks spent the afternoon being shown the Bay area by his old shipmate's wife. I'm sure this didn't seem a particularly unusual arrangement to Jack. He also had Jacqueline spend the first several weeks after their honeymoon at the Cape with his family. Their house wasn't ready in Washington, and, besides, the demands upon his time as a Senator were monumental. So the logical temporary place to stay seemed to Jack to be the Cape, where he would be every weekend. This again could not be rated as the top choice of a young bride for starting out making a home for her husband.

There is no question that the demands of public life placed

163

an unusual strain on the marriage of these two bright, attractive young people. Gossipmongers wanted to interpret the slightest deviation from what "newly married Town Square U.S.A." would do as a telltale sign of unrest. From my distant perch, the problems of Jack and Jacqueline Kennedy were about as serious as those of Anita and Red Fay, and I know few people who are better suited to live together as man and wife. It's not always the Garden of Eden, but, man, it is a lot of fun.

The day after my first meeting with Jacqueline, I asked Jack, "Why don't we slip over to the golf club and get in eighteen?"

Almost across the street from Hammersmith Farm were the green fairways of the Newport Country Club, where I had often played during the war. The gentry of Newport had opened up their club for the men in uniform, but with the end of the war the doors had shut tight again.

Jack looked at me, half tempted and half resigned. "Can't you see how well it will be received by the hopeful bride and her sheltering mother if the ardent husband-to-be spends his first day at her home playing golf with some old wartime buddy? For the sake of future marital bliss and cordial mother-in-law relationship, I'll forgo the privilege of watching that big game of yours. John Galvin will be up here this morning and you two can play."

When John arrived—that is, Boston John Galvin, not Dirty John—Jack drove us over to the club. Although none of us were members, Jack just said, "We'd like to get in a fast eighteen holes. Which will be the fastest, the front or the back nine?" And he added, "We'll need a couple of caddies." Although I sensed a slight undercurrent of tension among the old retainers, no one volunteered any interpretation of the rules.

Jack himself hit a couple of drives off the first tee, then watched us tee off. John Galvin, looking more Irish than Paddy's Pig, with me not far behind him, led off with a screaming hook. We were no sooner off than Jack returned to Hammersmith Farm.

When John and I reached the eighteenth hole, the Senator was waiting for us. He hustled us into his convertible and remarked, not without a touch of enjoyment, "I hope you two enjoyed your game of golf because as a result of it there was almost a total breakdown of relations between the mother of the bride and her dashing prospective son-in-law. It seems that there is a rule that nonmembers can play only when accompanied by a member there to sanction the match. I'm afraid that they feel that their worst fears are being realized. The invasion by the Irish Catholic hordes into one of the last strongholds of America's socially elite is being led by two chunky red-haired friends of the groom."

When Jack and I returned from my first visit to Hammersmith Farm ten days or so before his wedding, someone asked me what I thought of it.

"It was fantastic," I said. "That beautiful big place. In this day and age I don't know how anyone can afford to run anything that large. It was like getting a glimpse of Newport at its grandest before the era of the high income tax."

The wedding party shifted from Hyannis Port to Newport several days before the wedding. We were all farmed out to different homes, but then reconvened at Bailey's Beach for a touch football game and a swim.

The lifeguard, obviously a Democrat, said, "I want to tell you, this is the first time this place has had any life in it since I've been here."

During our game, Senator Theodore Green of Rhode Island walked along the edge of the beach near the cabanas. A polite, gracious little gentleman, then in his mid-eighties, he was extending a friendly greeting to everyone, oblivious of the game of football. At the same time, Teddy Kennedy, oblivious of Senator Green, was going out for a pass. They were on collision course. Everybody screamed.

Teddy, not knowing what the yelling was about, raced on—all 205 pounds at full speed. He missed Senator Green by a hair's breadth. If he had hit him, he would have driven him right into the concrete wall, and most likely that would have been the end of the good Senator. But Senator Green never knew how close a call he had. Like Mr. Magoo, he went right on greeting everybody as if nothing had happened.

A second bachelor dinner was held at Newport, with Hugh D. Auchincloss, the stepfather of the bride, as the host. This was to be a black-tie affair at the Clambake Club, one of the exclusive Newport retreats. As I'd had three sisters married by then, Jack said, "You know what the protocol is on this sort of an affair. You handle the job of master of ceremonies."

"There is really only one thing to keep in mind," I said. "That is for you to be sure to offer the first toast to the bride. And when the glasses are drained, no one should drink out of them again. They should be thrown into the fireplace."

Jack nodded.

At the party, he stood up and said solemnly, "Gentlemen,

166

I want you all to rise and drink a toast to my lovely bride."
All the guests stood up and drained their glasses.

Then Jack said, "Into the fireplace. We will not drink out of these glasses again."

All sixteen or eighteen guests tossed their glasses into the fireplace.

A shaken host, Hugh D. Auchincloss, who almost by reflex threw his glass along with the rest, called the waiter to replace the glasses.

As soon as the new crystal glasses were on the table, Jack rose again from his chair.

"Maybe this isn't the accepted custom," he said, "but I want to again express my love for this girl I'm going to marry. A toast to the bride."

Everyone joined in the toast again, and once again the crystal glasses flew into the fireplace.

By this time, an almost stunned Hugh D. had had enough. When the next set of glasses came in, they could have fitted very nicely into the rack at Healy's ten-cent restaurant.

Several nights later we were back at the Clambake Club— this time in the large dining room for the dinner given by the groom's family for the bridal party.

The ushers knew there would be many toasts, and most of them had given a few thoughts to what they would say if they were called on. Chuck Spalding, who had written a very successful book about flight training during the war—one of the most humorous books I have ever read—and had also written for Broadway shows, spent a good part of the afternoon preparing for his toast.

When the time came, Chuck gave a toast that could best be measured by the obvious appreciation of his old pal, the groom-to-be.

When my turn came, I took Ernest Thayer's "Casey at the Bat," substituted Jack for Casey, Newport for Mudville, and the names of the members of the bridal party for the other characters in the poem. My effort was almost completely without originality, but caught a measure of laughs.

After the dinner, Jack said to me, "Fay, how you continue to get away with the corn you pass out at parties is beyond me. Here Spalding gets up, makes what Arthur Krock told me he thought was one of the wittiest, brightest toasts he has ever heard. And you saw what sort of a reception it got. Then you have the raw guts to stand on your feet and do a take-off on 'Casey at the Bat,' and you're greeted as though you are a combination of Tennyson and Georgie Jessel. Spalding should have been cheered and you gotten what any poetic bandit deserves."

"Senator," I said, still full of myself, "it's all in the delivery."

Then, obviously feeling sorry for Chuck, Jack remarked sadly, "I'll tell you, something like this is going to crush Spalding." He went to search him out.

Jack brought Jacqueline west during their honeymoon, and Anita and I spent some time with them on the Monterey Peninsula. Then the four of us drove up to San Francisco in my little Ford convertible.

Jack and I agreed that we had to stop at Palo Alto to see Sergeant Tom Casey, whom Jack had first met when the UN was being formed, just before the end of World War II. The Sarge, who got his stripes in World War I, was almost a legendary figure around Stanford University. He had become the grounds keeper at the Palo Alto Municipal Center by the time Jack met him.

We drove around Palo Alto a few minutes, looking for the Sarge, and suddenly saw him just a little way ahead of us. With his baseball cap on, he was making his way to the baseball park to announce the day's game.

The Sarge is a little nearsighted, and this once prompted him to yell, "Go for three, kid," when a batter hit a long, wide foul down the left field line. When we got within earshot of his short, chubby figure, I yelled, "Case!"

He spun around, not seeing us immediately, and called out, "Kid, kid, where are you?"

Then he spotted the Senator. Suddenly the Sarge's arm was jabbing the air as though he were addressing a mass meeting. "The great Senator from the Commonwealth of Massachusetts," he shouted, as though introducing Jack to the gathered multitude, "one of this nation's greatest leaders—proved himself on foreign soil."

For some reason, Jack never forgot that phrase. Years later, when he could find the proper context for it in a speech, and probably because he knew of my love for the Sarge, out would come those words: "proved himself on foreign soil."

During the 1956 Presidential campaign, Jack came out to San Francisco to speak on behalf of Adlai Stevenson at the Fairmont Hotel. He must have received something over two hundred telegrams of welcome and encouragement before the dinner. He read just two: one from Stevenson and one from

Sergeant Tom Casey, who wasn't feeling well and wired his regrets for missing Jack's speech.

On the same visit to the coast which renewed Jack's acquaintance with the Sarge, he agreed to drop by my old fraternity house, the Zete House at Stanford. This was a Sunday early in October, and I felt sure some of the brothers of the old Mu chapter would be around.

As we walked up the stairs, I told Jack, "You'll find as fine a group of men in this house as you could find anyplace in the country. They'll be interested in meeting you, and they'll want to get your opinion on a lot of current issues."

I swung open the big oaken door which our class had given to the house on graduation, and we found ourselves looking at the back of a television set. The World Series was on, and about twenty of the brothers were glued to the tube.

For some reason, I thought that the entrance of the Senator from Massachusetts would cause all the loungers to jump to their feet and come rushing forward, eager to begin a penetrating survey of world problems.

Not a soul moved.

Finally I saw one member I knew, and I called him by name. Struggling to his feet, he came out past the television set to greet us.

"Bill, I'd like you to meet Senator Kennedy," I said. "Jack, this is Bill Tarr, the star fullback." I had to raise my voice slightly to make it register over the noise of the television set.

After Bill had acknowledged the introduction, I told him, "Bill, I'm sure the rest of the house would like to meet the Senator. Would you take care of the introductions?"

Bill, obviously surprised by the request, turned toward the

170

men, who were still staring at the television set, and yelled: "Hey, fellows, this is Senator Kennedy."

A few half-lifted themselves from their seats, and almost in unison they called, "Hi, Senator!" Then they went right back to the ball game.

Humiliated, angry and embarrassed, I said good-bye to Bill and we went out the door and down the stairs.

"I must say that was an alert group," Jack said as we left the Zete House. "It makes a difference to be able to meet so many Stanford Zetes at one time."

CHAPTER SEVENTEEN

N JANUARY, 1955, Bobby called me to ask if I could come to Florida. The family was worried about Jack, and didn't know whether he was going to live. The doctor felt that he was losing interest, and a visit from someone closely associated with happier times might help him regain his usual optimism and enjoyment of life.

I flew to Palm Beach and spent ten days with Jack. One of his crosses was the need to give himself medicine daily. Luckily, this was a treatment he had to endure only for a short period.

"Jack," I said, "the way you take that jab, it looks like it doesn't even hurt."

Before I had time to dodge, he reached over and jabbed the same needle into my leg. I screamed with the pain.

"It feels the same way to me," he commented flatly.

He couldn't sit or lie down in one position long because of the constant pain in his back. Despite the discomfort, he would force himself to sit still for a while each morning and each afternoon to read, always taking notes on the books which interested him. During that period, as I remember, he was reading some of the writings of Winston Churchill. After an hour or two of reading, he would take time to memorize some of the passages he had copied down. In fifteen or twenty minutes, he would memorize three or four pages of notes. Seven or eight years later I heard him quote verbatim some of the passages I knew he had read and memorized during that winter period in Florida.

A couple of days after I arrived, Jack felt well enough to go to a movie. We slid in behind the wheel of Mr. Kennedy's big Chrysler and drove over to West Palm Beach to catch Gary Cooper and Burt Lancaster in *Vera Cruz*. No one I knew liked to go to movies more than Jack, even though you had to stand at the "ready" to depart if he didn't like the film, which was not infrequent. If the action abated or the dialogue dragged, it was best to be ready to hear, "All right, let's haul it out of here."

After I had been at Palm Beach ten days, my sister telephoned to tell me that my father was critically ill. I told Jack that I had to return to California as quickly as possible, and he immediately took command.

"Redhead," he said, "Dad's secretary can make all arrangements and get you out on the next connection."

I ran up to my room and started packing. A few minutes later, Jack called from the bottom of the stairs, "Red, grab your things. They're holding a connecting plane at West Palm Beach."

Dave, the chauffeur, had the Fleetwood, engine running, standing at the front entrance. On the way to the car I told Jack, "If it is a matter of minutes, I'd like to drive. Can you handle Dave?"

He nodded.

At the car he simply said, "Dave, Red's driving."

Expecting to say good-bye to Jack right there, I turned to thank him. But he said, "Get in and start driving. I'm going with you."

The minute I got the car on the road and felt the bare response to the steering in the tropical rainstorm I knew the tires were smooth. Jack could feel the uncertainty also and said, "For Christ's sake, Dave, how could you let the tires get down that smooth? We'll be lucky to get to the airport without an accident. Please see that these tires are changed this afternoon." Poor Dave, already replaced by an amateur, was having a bad day.

We held our breath at every turn and intersection until our luck ran out at the entrance to the airport. We hit a slick spot and the car started spinning. We made a complete circle, but luckily ended up unhurt and headed in the right direction.

At the airport building, several officials of the airline grabbed my bags and advised me to hurry.

"So long, Jack," I said. "Many thanks."

With that great smile, he called, "Redhead, you were the

difference. Even Dave hates to see you go. Now he'll have to drive home alone with me."

A smile crossed Dave's face. He knew he was forgiven.

I ran up the ramp to the plane. The door closed behind me, and the plane immediately taxied out and took off. Obviously, the word had gone out from Joseph P. Kennedy that that plane was not to take off until I was on it.

On the sixth or seventh of February, I received a letter of thanks from the Senator. "That was a nice ride to the airport," he wrote. "Doc Muskin took my blood pressure two hours later—it was up about 20 points from the day before. He said with his unerring accuracy, 'You're really getting better. It's amazing.' "

Jack slowly regained his health, but it wasn't until Dr. Janet Travell had taken some positive remedial measures that he started to enjoy the level of health that made his race for the Presidency possible.

In 1957 I was having some trouble with my shoulder as a result of an old touch football injury, and Jack said, "Listen, I have a doctor who has done absolute wonders with me. I credit her with getting me back on my feet. She will cure you. I'll call her right now."

Within minutes I had an appointment for late that afternoon. Then, with a faint trace of pleasure, the Senator proceeded to tell me how she worked her marvels. He said she drove a long hollow needle into the muscle and flooded it with novocaine, which caused the muscle to relax. When the trauma passed, all the ligaments would start pulling together, he said, rather than leaning on the strength of a contiguous muscle.

175

"After a little of Doc Travell you'll know what I've been going through for the past few years," he said.

I went to Dr. Travell's office and was immediately placed in a chair and stripped to the waist. Almost as quickly, one of the longest injection needles I have ever seen was waving in front of my face. Dr. Travell couldn't have been more understanding and professional, but I was human.

The first injections were made around the top of the shoulder. I was bearing up quite well until she told me: "Please raise your arm, we have to come up through the armpit."

I was now in a cold sweat. But as soon as that injection had been made, I got a reprieve. The phone rang.

The good doctor excused herself and answered it. I couldn't quite grasp the conversation, as she was in another room, but I could tell she was enjoying the discussion because of her laughter.

The conversation concluded, Dr. Travell came back in. "That was Senator Kennedy," she said. "He wanted to know if you had cried or screamed."

After about an hour of torture, the doctor said, "That is all for now, Mr. Fay, but you will need another treatment tomorrow morning to get really satisfactory results." Then, shifting to another gear, she added: "That will be one hundred dollars for today's treatment."

I was stunned.

"I had no idea the cost would be so high," I replied. "I'm not questioning the possible success of your treatment, but I couldn't afford to come again tomorrow at that price."

As I peeled off a hundred-dollar bill—a sizable portion of

my trip money—Dr. Travell said, "You are being charged no more than I charge Senator Kennedy and his brothers."

"Unfortunately for me," I said, "what the Kennedys can afford and what I can afford are two different things. Thank you for what you have done, but I can't come tomorrow. I'll just have to hope that today's treatment will do the trick."

The doctor said, "You come back tomorrow morning. You need the treatment. There will be no charge."

One day Bob Tallman, who was then the assistant to the president of Transamerica, asked me to intercede with the Senator from Massachusetts about the Bank Holding Act of 1956, which Transamerica considered unfair.

I knew nothing about the merits of Transamerica's arguments, but I told Bob I would be happy to give him a letter of introduction to the Senator, simply stating that he was a friend of mine whom I could handle easily on the basketball court. The rest would be up to him.

An intense, hard-driving man, Bob went to Washington, saw Evelyn Lincoln and Ted Sorensen, and then had an interview with Jack. I'm sure that Bob was forceful, and Jack was undoubtedly attentive—listening, as always, in an open, friendly manner, but avoiding any commitment. Bob followed up his visit by sending along material in support of his position.

When the bill reached the floor of the Senate, Jack's vote was in opposition to Transamerica's position. Bob rang me up to tell me that my friend had double-crossed him.

I wrote to Jack, reporting Tallman's reaction, and received this reply:

"Red, I'm sorry that your friend got so upset, but I'm afraid he mistook a warm smile and a firm handshake for an indication of active support."

In 1959, Jack Kennedy agreed to go out to Hawaii to campaign for John Burns, who was running on the Democratic ticket against Territorial Governor Bill Quinn for the position of first Governor of the State of Hawaii.

Jack called me and asked if I would like to make the trip with him. After a fairly major job of selling at home, I got a pass and told the Senator I was with him. We were supposed to meet in Los Angeles and fly out together, but he was delayed. I ended up flying out in the same plane with Steve and Jean Smith, landing in Honolulu several hours before the Senator.

Along with what seemed to be about half the population of the islands, I went out to greet the Senator. It was just after sunrise, but the crowd was shouting and cheering.

On Jack's arrival, hula girls heaped lei after lei over his head till he could hardly see his benefactors.

Ramrod-straight, tough, cold, chiseled-looking John Burns stepped forward to greet the Senator. With such a tumultuous welcome, I wondered if Burns hesitated to ponder just who was the candidate. As soon as the Senator could work his way through the crowd, he was escorted to a VIP room for coffee and rolls to meet the leading Democrats of the Territory.

We hadn't been in the room more than ten minutes when a very harassed-looking man came up to the Democratic Party chairman and blurted, "Quinn is coming in here to welcome

178

the Senator." The Democratic leader exploded. "He has a lot of nerve to come here."

Before another word could be spoken, in walked the Republican Party candidate for Governor. He came right up to the Senator and in an affable, open, friendly manner stated, "Senator, not only as Hawaii's Territorial Governor but as an admirer of yours, let me welcome you to Honolulu." He handled himself so graciously and with such good manners he was a standout. It was obvious that Jack enjoyed meeting him, a fact which caused consternation in the Democratic ranks. When Quinn left and Jack had a chance to speak to me, he whispered, "You have to admire a guy like Quinn. He was absolutely right in coming here in spite of the poor welcome." Then, as if thinking out loud, he leaned over, continuing: "From what you have seen so far of the two candidates which would you choose for Governor? Burns or Quinn?" Before I could answer, he whispered, "Mine is Quinn."

When the gathering broke up, Jack and I were led by Bill Richardson, who seemed to be in authority, through the airport to waiting limousines. Just before we reached the cars, a reporter with a tape recorder prevailed upon Jack to give an interview.

After answering a few questions and looking for a way out, the Senator turned to me as I stood, happily secure in my anonymity, and said to the reporter, "Have you met Congressman Fay?"

I couldn't believe my ears.

"What district are you from, Congressman?" the reporter asked.

My answer must have sounded a little suspicious.

"Oh, I'm from one of the California districts," I said.

Not content to drop what had all the earmarks of a fruitless interview, the reporter pushed on: "Congressman, do you feel that Senator Kennedy will be a strong favorite with the Democratic Party for the Presidential nomination in 1960?"

Feeling that I could easily field that, I started to reply. As the words started to pour out, I happened to catch the eye of the Senator. He was giving me a look of shocked horror. Suddenly I saw myself in a few short words destroying Jack's Presidential chances. Right in the middle of my response, my words became an unintelligible array of syllables eventually trailing off into a weak mumble.

The reporter, with good justification and a look of disbelief, terminated the interview. I stepped into the limousine with the Senator feeling that I had just given an excellent demonstration of a man with a collapsed mind. The Senator, having obviously enjoyed my dilemma, commented, "There goes another American—" referring to the reporter—"confident that his government is in good hands."

With Jack's candidacy for the Democratic nomination now widely recognized, there were persistent idle rumors that Jack and Jacqueline were suffering marital differences. One day in 1960 while he and I were playing golf at Cypress Point Club, I decided to ask him about a rumor I had heard.

"The sister of the wife of one of my closest friends, who supposedly travels in the same set in New York as Jackie and Lee, has circulated the story that Jackie is staying with you only until you are nominated or the election is over, and then is going to divorce you," I told him. "She claims she got the information from one of Jackie's closest friends. I want the rebuttal directly from you, so I can kill the story at its source."

Jack looked at me calmly as though I had just told him that his shoe was untied.

"Red," he said, without a flicker, "the story is false, but I wouldn't feel all that confident about killing it if I were you. People who spread stories like that don't want to accept a denial. I think I know the girl in New York who is spreading that report. She and Jackie go to some of the same parties, and, amazingly enough, Jackie says she is always very friendly."

Actually, the White House probably drew them closer together than they had ever been before. The roles of President and First Lady tended to demand that they stand apart from others, which in turn gave them many more hours together. Since their roles complemented each other in so many ways, Jack did a poor job of trying to conceal his pride in Jacqueline's accomplishments as First Lady.

He was not a demonstrative husband in public, and was rarely seen by others kissing or embracing his wife. But the pride and love were obvious to anyone who saw them together, particularly during the Presidential years.

I remember one evening at Squaw Island in the summer of 1963. It was about 7:30, but it was still daylight on the Cape, and the weather was mild. As the four of us talked, Jack, Jacqueline, Anita and I, Jacqueline was sketching the furniture arrangements for the rooms in their new home in Middleburg, Virginia.

Jack and Jacqueline had received several Grecian and Roman busts and small statuettes, and were about to decide which ones to keep and which to return. Jack was attracted by a very small metal statuette, perhaps four or five inches tall, which was supposedly nearly two thousand years old. The price seemed very high to me.

"How do you know you're not being taken?" I asked. "Maybe this little statue was made at a hobby shop a couple of weeks ago."

"Ask Jackie," Jack said.

I looked skeptical, and I was, because I had not thought of Jacqueline as an authority on classical statuettes.

"Ask Jackie any question you can think of dealing with Roman or Greek history and she will give you the answers," Jack said. "Then ask her about the authenticity of this figurine."

Since I had barely managed to squeeze through Latin in high school and had a very vague grasp of Greek history, I replied, "I'm not going to be much of a quizzer because I couldn't confirm or deny any of the answers."

Jack took over. With obvious pride he started quizzing Jacqueline, using a book on Greek history as his source for questions.

At first she hesitated. "Jack, this is ridiculous," she said. "How are my answers going to prove how old that Grecian statue is?"

Jack persisted, and Jacqueline began answering. It was an amazing performance. She obviously had had no opportunity to prepare herself ahead of time, but still she answered every question with ease.

The next day Jack and I went over to have a swim in his father's swimming pool at the main house. I commented on

President toasts Under Secretary of the Navy at his birthday party aboard the Sequoia *in July, 1963.*

Hyannis Port Country Club, Summer, 1963.

a cheerful loser
happy winner —

John Kennedy

JFK makes a White House visit a memorable occasion for Paul B. Fay III, his sister Katherine (center) and his cousin Joan Barry. Summer, 1963.

Another still from motion picture PT 109 inscribed by JFK for Barney Ross: " 'You mean you want me to tell Red Fay he's going to New Guinea' John Kennedy."

Still from motion picture PT 109 *inscribed by JFK for Barney Ross, who played role of a Navy chief instead of himself. "I'll get you Kennedy so help me God." John Kennedy."*

The President and First Lady watching America's Cup Races on board destroyer U.S.S. Joseph P. Kennedy, Jr. with Senator Ben Smith, Captain Tazewell Shepard, Under Secretary of Navy Paul B. Fay, Jr. and Hugh Auchincloss, stepfather of Mrs. Kennedy. Newport.

Nicole Alphand, the wife of the former Ambassador from France, with Robert Kennedy and Anita Fay. Navy Relief Ball, Fall, 1963.

Two proud fathers with their wonderful daughters flanking one of the Navy's best.

The President proves to Nice Al Webb, hat executive (right), that there is someone who looks worse in a hat than he does. White House President's Office, 1963.

Jacqueline's unbelievable performance the evening before, and then we began talking about wives in general. As if looking back over his adult years, he said, "I'd known a lot of attractive women in my lifetime before I got married, but of all of them there was only one I could have married—and I married her."

Because he was not demonstrative in public, some people did not realize how warm and compassionate Jack Kennedy could be to his family and friends. I remember one illustration of this one weekend up at Squaw Island on the Cape.

Although Jack and I had been close friends for years, this didn't mean that Jacqueline and Anita, or Caroline and my daughter, Sally, were going to be equally good friends. Occasionally a weekend together, while it might be a ball for Jack and myself, could be a great strain for the ladies and girls.

On this particular weekend after lunch I must have said something that tipped the scales, because Anita got up and left the room obviously hurt, not from what was said at that particular moment but from the accumulation of thoughtlessness by me over the weekend.

When Jack asked with concern, "Is she all right?" I replied in typical fatheaded husband fashion, "She'll get over it. If I sympathize with her, it will just exaggerate a minor incident."

Obviously not satisfied with my rationalization, Jack got up. "I'm going to speak to her," he said. "I don't think we've been as considerate of her feelings as we could have been."

He walked upstairs and found Anita in our room on top of her bed in tears. Sitting on the edge of the bed, he talked for about half an hour until she was finally settled down. With a few thoughtful words and moments, the President of the United States made my darling Bride feel like the Queen of the May. Somewhere well down among the knaves was the Queen of the May's husband.

CHAPTER EIGHTEEN

N SUNDAY EVENING, April 16, 1961, my wife and I went over to Bobby Kennedy's Hickory Hill home for a cookout.

We were all sitting on the grass behind the house when Bobby said, "Redhead, do you know that early tomorrow morning some Cuban patriots are landing in Cuba to try to overthrow Castro?"

Stunned, I replied, "No, Bob, never heard of it."

I felt humiliated because I had received no advance information. This became even more galling when I was told of the Navy's role in the landing. My personal pride was slightly re-established when the President told me later the operation was on a need-to-know basis.

But if I was suffering from injured pride, this was nothing compared to the agonizing frustration the President suffered after the disastrous fiasco at the Bay of Pigs. In the months that followed, no matter how you tried to avoid touching on the subject, by one route or another it seemed to find its way back into the President's conversation.

For a short while—probably not more than a few weeks— this experience even affected Jack's relish for the Presidency itself. One day that spring we were driving out to Middleburg, and as we came through the gate in front of the White House a number of people were standing near the entrance. Jack waved at the friendly crowd, but then he said to me, "By God, if they think they are going to get me to run for a second term, they're out of their minds. They can have this job when I finish my four years."

"Oh, what are you talking about?" I said. "Just because something disturbs you now . . . "

It was the only time I ever heard him discuss the possibility of bowing out after one term, and I'm certain that this was merely a reflection of his discouragement about the Bay of Pigs.

A few weeks later, Anita and I were weekend guests of the Robert Kennedys at Cape Cod. One evening the four of us went over to have dinner with the President and Jacqueline.

Jacqueline had hoped to have a pleasant, relaxing dinner, without any political talk and in particular any comments about the Bay of Pigs. She put me on one side of the President. Bobby sat next to me. During the main course, Bob, the President and I drifted inextricably into a discussion about the

186

military, and then the Bay of Pigs. Jacqueline, Anita and Ethel were trying to carry on a lighter conversation, but as the President became more and more serious and intense, they fell into a kind of hush.

As we got up after dinner, Jacqueline said to me, "You know, I had hoped we were going to have a pleasant dinner, instead of having Jack go through another one of those sessions on the Bay of Pigs."

Then Jacqueline, Anita, Ethel and Bob left to go to the movies over at the big house. The President and I were left alone.

"Why don't we play some backgammon?" he said, still tense from the dinner conversation.

"I really don't know how to play backgammon," I replied lamely. "How about some dominoes?"

With a note of disgust, he answered, "I don't know how to play dominoes, but I'm sure we both know how to play checkers."

He moved from the dining room to the living room on his crutches—a reminder of a tree-planting episode in Canada. We sat at a very small table. The checkerboard lapped over the sides of the table, and was supported partly by our knees.

I was winning the first game, when I noticed a warning look in his eyes. He coughed suddenly, and the checkerboard bounced, sending the checkers onto the floor or helter-skelter across the checkerboard.

"One of those unfortunate incidents of life, Redhead," he said with a touch of a smile. "We'll never really know if the Under Secretary was going to strategically outmaneuver the Commander in Chief."

We started in again. But now that brain had been sufficiently refreshed on the strategy of the game. Everything was fore-ordained. Regardless of what I did, he had me beaten.

After he won two games, Jack got back to the subject of the Bay of Pigs. He talked about critics who admonished him for not going into Cuba full force and taking over the country. As he spoke, his temper rose.

"Nobody is going to force me to do anything I don't think is in the best interest of this country," he said. "I will never compromise the principles on which this country is built, but we're not going to plunge into an irresponsible action just because a fanatical fringe in this country puts so-called national pride above national reason.

"Do you think I'm going to carry on my conscience the responsibility for the wanton maiming and killing of children like our children we saw here this evening? Do you think I'm going to cause a nuclear exchange—for what? Because I was forced into doing something that I didn't think was proper and right? Well, if you or anybody else thinks I am, he's crazy."

He got up and reached for his crutches. I knew he was finished with me for the evening. He started up the stairs, straining with every step. He stopped in the middle of the stairs and looked down at me his face still inflamed.

"By God, there will be no avoiding responsibility nor will there be any irresponsibility. When the decisive time for action arrives, action will be taken."

Turning, he lifted himself painfully up the rest of the stairs and to his room.

It was a lonely, troubled President who sought solace in his thoughts. I felt a sudden flush of pride and admiration for my President, a reassurance that he could never be forced to act irrationally, no matter how many angry, frightened people might try to influence him. He would make up his own mind, coolly and unemotionally.

The fiasco in Cuba raised strong doubts in his mind about the intelligence and judgment of some of the top military men.

"Looking back on that whole Cuban mess, one of the things that appalled me most was the lack of broad judgment by some of the heads of the military services," he said one day. "When you think of the long competitive selection process that they have to weather to end up the number one man of their particular service, it is certainly not unreasonable to expect that they would also be bright, with good broad judgment. For years I've been looking at those rows of ribbons and those four stars, and conceding a certain higher qualification not obtained in civilian life. Well, if ——— and ——— are the best the services can produce, a lot more attention is going to be given their advice in the future before any action is taken as a result of it. They wanted to fight and probably calculated that if we committed ourselves part way and started to lose, I would give the okay to pour in whatever was needed. I found out among other things that when it comes to making decisions I want facts more than advice. As good old Harry Truman put it, 'the buck stops right here.' I can see now why McNamara wants to get some new faces over there in the Pentagon."

Between the Bay of Pigs and the Cuban missile crisis, Fletcher Knebel and Charles W. Bailey, II brought out a book, *Seven Days in May,* which explored the possibility of a take-over by the military in this country. Mrs. John R. Fell, an old

189

friend of the Kennedys, had read an advance copy of the book and recommended it to the President one summer weekend in 1962, during an afternoon sail on the *Honey Fitz.*

"I'd be interested to see if you agree that such a situation could develop in this country," she said.

"Fletch sent me a copy, but I haven't gotten around to reading it," the President said. "I'll read it tonight and let you know."

We were out on the *Honey Fitz* again the next day, and the President said he had read *Seven Days in May* the previous night. He discussed the possibility of such a military takeover very calmly:

"It's possible. It could happen in this country, but the conditions would have to be just right. If, for example, the country had a young President, and he had a Bay of Pigs, there would be a certain uneasiness. Maybe the military would do a little criticizing behind his back, but this would be written off as the usual military dissatisfaction with civilian control. Then if there were another Bay of Pigs, the reaction of the country would be, 'Is he too young and inexperienced?' The military would almost feel that it was their patriotic obligation to stand ready to preserve the integrity of the nation, and only God knows just what segment of democracy they would be defending if they overthrew the elected establishment."

As if steeling himself for the final challenge, he continued, "Then, if there were a third Bay of Pigs, it could happen."

Pausing long enough for all of us to assess the significance of his comment, he concluded with an old Navy phrase: "But it won't happen on my watch."

As hard as the Bay of Pigs disaster was for him to accept,

it marked a dramatic change in his growth as a President. If he had unconsciously shared the mantle of responsibility before, he did no longer. His decisive, precise, brilliant handling of the Cuban missile crisis was the impressive example of a President in complete control of the enormous powers of his office.

After his television appearance on that fateful Monday evening when the whole world held its breath, I wrote him a note.

"Mr. President," I said, "last night after your television appearance I was one of millions of Americans who were proud and confident in a way that a man seldom has the opportunity to experience. Last night without reservations you were our Commander in Chief."

It seemed that my note had hardly been picked up from my "out box" before the receptionist called me. "Mr. Secretary, the President is calling," she said.

"Red, I wanted to thank you for your note," the President said, "and also to tell you of the magnificent manner in which the military conducted themselves throughout this whole period. They all knew, if word leaked out, that my appearance on television last night could have been negated by a Russian charge that we were going to spread wild stories of supposed missiles in Cuba. There were hundreds of military men that had to be brought in, but there wasn't one leak. On top of that, when I asked them if we had to go into Cuba to remove the missiles, could we do it, there wasn't one dissenting voice. It is awfully reassuring to have that kind of support."

Then, in closing: "Thanks, Old Lovable, I appreciate your note."

When the connection broke, my eyes were filled with tears.

Tears because my President had grown so that now the military leaders who had once been held responsible for part of his private frustration after the Bay of Pigs were again seen in their proper position. He was now asking them for information more than for counsel.

But it was also an indication of the greatness of the President of the United States that he took time for the simple, thoughtful, human act of ringing up to say "thanks."

There is no mystery why he was loved.

CHAPTER NINETEEN

HEN THERE WAS no major crisis, John Kennedy could spend a weekend at the Cape in complete relaxation, enjoying life and his family with the same concentration that he gave during the week to the duties of the Presidency.

Sailing, swimming, playing with John, Jr. and Caroline or just being with Jacqueline, he would seem totally cut off from the responsibilities of his office, although he spent several hours each weekend morning keeping up with governmental matters.

Early Monday morning, he was instantly absorbed in his work again. He always seemed eager to get back to the problems he knew he would face at the White House.

When he boarded the helicopter, all the newspapers were ready for him, and he would start going through them before the noisy propellers lifted the craft from the ground.

I've never seen anyone else read a newspaper quite the way John Kennedy did. He folded the page lengthwise, a custom followed by some people on a crowded subway. But then his eyes would sweep down the columns at an incredible speed. When he came to something that particularly interested him, he would read the entire article, still at breakneck speed, and would retain the details almost completely.

One morning he focused on an article by Scotty Reston. I could see his irritation as he read it, and then he shoved the article over to me and said, "Read that."

This was not a Presidential order that I relished. When I first came to Washington, my reading speed was about 400 words a minute. I took a speed-reading course, and I got it up to about 800 words a minute, with about 90 percent comprehension. But I knew that the President read around 2,200 or 2,400 words a minute, with almost total comprehension.

He waited impatiently for me to read the Reston column. Of course, it's always worse when sombody is waiting for you to read something. Rushing beyond my real capacity, I was probably going about 1,200 words a minute with about 2 percent comprehension. All I wanted to do was to get the general gist of it. But when I was about halfway through, he said in an irritated tone, "What are you trying to do, memorize it?"

This pulverized my concentration, and I might as well have been reading a blank page. Finally I reread it and was able to speak about the contents of the article. Under the Presidential marking system, good old Scotty Reston failed the course that day.

Another weekend he read an article by Drew Pearson describing an incident which was supposed to indicate that the President was bored to tears because he had to have Peter Lawford around.

"That Pearson," he said. "The whole article is a lie."

Then, in a mood of sadness, he added: "It's so unfair. Now that Peter and Pat are having a rough time, this is just plain cruel. Here I am, President of the United States, and I can't do anything to stop somebody like Pearson."

The President liked Peter Lawford, and his inherent kindness was always apparent when he thought one of his friends had been treated shabbily.

I never knew just when he was going to be upset by a particular magazine or newspaper. One week it might be *Time* and another the New York *Herald Tribune,* but he was almost always strongly critical of *U.S. News & World Report*—not of the entire contents, but of what he thought was biased reporting.

One weekend up at the Cape, we were walking from Bob's house to his. I just happened to have a copy of *Time* in my hand. He noticed the magazine and reacted as though I were a traitor to the New Frontier.

"What are you doing carrying *that* magazine around?" he asked.

Faking stunned disbelief that I had such a publication in my hand, I flung it into the bushes as if shaking off a deadly viper.

"My God, how could I have ever done such a thing?" I exclaimed. "I must be losing my mind."

He smiled—mostly at himself for his brash question. I then remembered that that issue of *Time* included a particularly unflattering article about the President.

Time did have its good weeks around the White House, but that was not so much the case with David Lawrence's magazine, *U.S. News & World Report.* One issue I remember particularly featured a full-scale article about the President's planes, helicopters, automobiles and all the other transportation and communications facilities.

"Look what they say," Jack steamed. "My God, when you read that article it sounds as if I were the first President to have planes, helicopters and cars to get around in. The whole article is an attempt to discredit."

I was amused at Jack's strong reaction. I am convinced that the average American doesn't think twice about how many cars, planes and boats the President has. He is the President of the United States, and whatever he needs, that's what he should have.

"Mr. President," I said, "it's the same old story. You're too close to the issue. The only people who are going to get exercised by an article like that are the people who would be against you anyway. The President of the United States is the number one man in this country and the people are proud to have him travel in style."

I didn't seem to convince him.

"Thanks, Grand Old Lovable," he said. "You do bring an aura of the grass roots to the seat of government."

If my recollection is accurate, about the time that article appeared, a much closer control was put on the people eligible to ride to Hyannis Port on the President's plane. Before, it seemed that everyone who was anyone in Washington would get clearance to go on the plane. When we climbed into the sky, it was a happy commuter plane crowded with children and wives going away to the Cape for the weekend, with the President in many cases the unknowing host. After the crackdown, all passengers had to obtain advance approval from the "Ice Man," Kenny O'Donnell.

One of the President's frequent guests aboard the Presidential plane was Dean Markham. Dean, like so many other young men of the New Frontier, came to Washington at a great personal sacrifice. In his case he took a cut in pay of over 50 percent but can look back over his period of service to John Kennedy and his country with pride in accomplishment.

I happened to mention to the President one day an item that Dean wanted to have brought to his attention. "Tell me," the President said. "What is Dean Markham like? It seems that every time I open the door of Air Force One to look back into the plane to see who is on board, there is Dean Markham. It's almost the same in the White House Executive Wing. I round a corner and there is Dean Markham. The Administration is still young and already Dean Markham is almost a legendary figure." To this day, Dean still does consultant work at the White House. He is a legendary figure.

In December of 1961, John Connally resigned as Secretary of the Navy to run for Governor of Texas, and was succeeded by Fred Korth, who was also from Fort Worth.

Fred could not assume the position until January, 1962, and then had to wait three or four weeks for security clearance. During this period, I was Acting Secretary of the Navy.

While I was Acting Secretary, the President called a National Security Council meeting. I arrived about twenty minutes early, to be sure nothing could deprive me of the privilege of attending. Bob McNamara also arrived early. Knowing the high esteem in which the President held him, I was surprised to observe McNamara's apparent nervousness. The only explanation I could offer for it was his eagerness to do an excellent job for someone he likewise admired greatly.

As only Cabinet officers and a few key advisers sat at the main Cabinet table, I took my position at a chair along the wall, next to FBI Director J. Edgar Hoover. I had met Mr. Hoover only once before, but we chatted along easily for about ten minutes.

Suddenly the door in the direction of the President's office opened and he walked in without fanfare. Instantly, everyone stood in silence. As he walked the few strides to his seat at the center of the table, he spotted me. Breaking his course, he turned and walked up to Mr. Hoover and me. With that smile in his eyes, he asked, "Mr. Director, do you know the Under Secretary of the Navy?"

"Why, Mr. President," Mr. Hoover said, "Red and I are old friends."

The President cut in with that special fast-curing needle: "Obviously, you have never looked up his record."

With the head of the FBI left speechless—no mean feat in itself—the President went on to his seat to conduct a memorable National Security Council meeting. He reviewed without using any notes, in a very personal, conversational manner the successes and failures of the past year. He compared the problems the Soviet Union and the United States faced in winning the alliance of the new and struggling countries of the world. For the Soviets, he said, the task "is relatively simple once they get control, because they force the overtaken country into a controlled state which conforms or succumbs. But we have to deal with all levels of democracy—some of which are far from what we consider democracy in this country. The gratifying thing is that we are slowly gaining where they are losing."

A few weeks after I became Under Secretary of the Navy, I found myself in the middle of a minor newspaper controversy.

It all started very quietly. When I arrived at the office one morning, one of my aides asked, "Mr. Secretary, did you read Marquis Childs' column this morning?"

"No, I very seldom read his column," I said.

"You'd better read it this morning," he said.

I read it, first with curiosity and then with amazement. Childs charged that I had tried to use my friendship with the President to get around the Defense Department's policy on clearing—or censoring—speeches. Childs reported that I had first tried to clear a speech by Vice Admiral Charlie Martell with Arthur Sylvester. When that failed, the columnist said, I had gone over Sylvester's head and had sought approval for the speech from the President himself.

In my naïveté, this seemed to me nothing more than an extreme example of poor reporting, and I put the column out of my mind, feeling that I had missed little by not reading Childs in the past.

Later that morning, Secretary of the Navy Connally called me in.

"Red, I want you to know that I read the Childs article and Bob McNamara discussed it with me. I assured Bob that you hadn't tried to circumvent any of his policies to get a speech cleared."

"My God," I thought to myself, "if McNamara is talking to John about that damn column, they must be a bit concerned."

I was tempted to phone Childs to try to find out where he got such garbage, but I had other work to take care of and let it slip.

I was lunching alone in the Secretary of the Navy's dining room, still annoyed by the column, when the phone rang. I picked it up. A voice on the other end said, "One moment, please, for Mr. Marquis Childs."

I was dumfounded. My quarry was walking right into my grasp.

"Hello, Paul," the next voice said. (I'd met the columnist once in my life.) "This is Mark Childs. I wanted to get a little bit more information on that article I wrote this morning."

"You want to get more information for your article!" I exploded. "I'd like to know where you got the information that you used in your article today."

In an almost cavalier manner he replied, "Oh I got that from some of the admirals."

"You got it from some of the admirals!" I repeated. "Just tell me who the admirals were. The only admiral present was Admiral Dan Smith. Arthur Sylvester was there, his aide was there, and I was there. Now who'd you say you got it from? You didn't get it from Smith, that I know."

There was a momentary silence.

I started up again. "If this is the way you operate, it's a sad commentary on so-called leading columnists."

Then, obviously from another open extension of the phone, came the two words: "Bull Conn."

I was stopped dead. There was only one voice like that in America. It was John Kennedy's.

After a second he said, "God, I've never heard anybody get so worked up over one column. How would you like to get it every day in five or six newspapers like your old pal? I'm not sure that you are ready to take McNamara's place."

Then, just before hanging up, he said, "It's nice to know that we still have some loyal supporters over in the Pentagon."

I felt that the President must have wanted to get an answer if he went to all that trouble, so I decided to try to discover the source of Childs' charge.

After an exhaustive study, checked and rechecked through Admiral Dan Smith, Pierre Salinger and others, all the evidence pointed to Arthur Sylvester as the source of Childs' false report. Perhaps he believed that I was going to try to discredit him with the President, and his reaction was to strike first.

I wrote up a report on the whole incident, naming all the principals. By clearing all but one, I left the obvious conclusion that Arthur was the source of the Childs column. (Incidentally, I later grew to respect and like Arthur Sylvester more with each passing year.)

With all my facts in hand, I arrived at the President's office on Monday, April 17, 1961. I was waiting in Evelyn Lincoln's office when the President came out of his office. He spotted me and asked, "What do you want?" He looked tense and impatient.

"Mr. President," I replied, "here are the papers giving all the facts on the Marquis Childs incident."

He took them from my hand and glanced at them briefly, but not long enough to assimilate all the facts before breaking into a wan smile.

"Redhead, I want to ask you a simple question," he said. "Which do you think is more important to the President of the United States, getting the blow-by-blow account on how Red Fay cleared his record or trying to find some way of not getting our block completely knocked off in the Bay of Pigs?"

A thoroughly chastened Under Secretary of the Navy quietly crept back to the Pentagon. I had been so completely absorbed in my own little problem I had forgotten that only a few hours earlier the anti-Castro Cubans had landed at the Bay of Pigs.

While he took the Childs column calmly, his reaction to a blunder by the Marines' Public Information Office indicated how much importance he placed on newspapers and magazines. I was reading the newspapers back in the general passenger compartment of Air Force One when a Secret Service man came to tell me that the President wanted to see me back in his stateroom.

I found the President lying on his bunk with a copy of the *Saturday Evening Post* in his hand. He handed it to me.

"Red, is this the new Marine Corps image that you're promoting over in the Pentagon?"

A full-color illustration in the magazine showed Marines in full battle dress making a landing through surf. Lounging on well-placed rocks or reclining on a landing craft were models dressed in bathing suits exposing their torsos in varying degrees.

I had seen the article earlier, and had intended to find out who had been responsible for allowing such a promotion, but it had slipped my mind.

Before I could make a comment, he continued, "Red, I want to know who was responsible for clearing an article like this. Here the greatest fighting force in the world is selling out to publicize bathing suits."

Assuring the President I would get right on it, I left. In a matter of seconds, the power of the Presidency was starting to take effect. I got on the phone in the plane and soon was "patched" into the switchboard at the White House.

"Please call the Pentagon and get the Navy Chief of Public Information on the phone."

"I'll call you right back, Mr. Secretary," the operator replied.

Within a few minutes I was talking to the number two officer in that department. He informed me that the Admiral, in this case John McCain, was on leave. I told the officer about the President's reaction to the magazine article, and he said he would find out immediately who cleared it.

"I think I should notify the Admiral of the President's interest so that at least he will be abreast of what is going on," he said.

"You're absolutely correct," I said. "If Admiral McCain is going to take any lumps on this, he should be fully aware of the President's interest."

McCain cut short his leave and rushed back to Washington to be damn sure that not a detail was omitted from the report on the entire incident. When I returned to Washington on Monday, John McCain came pounding into my office, cigar at the ready, looking as though he should be on the bridge of a ship rather than wet-nursing PIO types (Public Information Officers).

"Mr. Secretary," he said, "I'm humiliated. Some damn PIO type who should be working for a fashion magazine instead of wearing a Navy uniform permitted this article with its pictures to be published without getting clearance. Please tell the President this won't happen again—at least, not from this gentleman."

The incident was closed, but the effect of the President's interest was amazing. Suddenly every man in the PIO section of the Navy had a feeling that if the President wasn't watching him personally at least he knew what he was doing.

Because of his recognition of the enormous influence of newspapers, and also the happy elite audience in attendance, the President gave a lot of thought to his first speech as President at the annual Gridiron Club dinner. Not thinking of himself, because the President spoke only briefly, he told me the impression a political figure made at this dinner could make or break him in political circles. He mentioned one politician with Presidential ambitions who had spoken at the dinner one year. "He did poorly and never was a contender after that." The tradition of the affair was to be critical in a partisan political vein but always with humor.

Thruston Morton, representing the Republican Party, spoke first. He delivered a bitter talk, completely devoid of humor, about the first hundred days of the Kennedy administration.

A pall fell over the crowd. The President had difficulty concealing his irritation. Then Eugene McCarthy got up to represent the Democratic Party. His was too much of an intellectual offering for a spirited occasion. It was humorous, but the humor was a little bit too sophisticated.

Then it was time for the President. Seldom has anyone taken such sheer delight as he did in making that speech. Everyone was roaring. I'd always thought of Sam Rayburn as a bald-headed fellow with a scowl on his face. That evening he laughed so hard at John Kennedy that his whole head was purple, the tears running down his face.

As I was leaving after the dinner, I ran into Henry Ford. In his usual generous manner he said, "Come on upstairs with me. Sidney Weinberg's holding forth in his suite. All the fellows will be there."

Up we went. "The fellows" were the industrial leaders of the country, known to me only by reputation.

Henry couldn't have been nicer introducing me, but I didn't find too much in common with the other guests. Besides, I like to do my drinking before dinner. After twenty minutes or so I caught Henry's eye and said, "Henry I'm going to slip out. Many thanks."

He pulled himself away from his group and said, "Wait a minute, Red. I want to walk down to the elevator with you."

When we got out in the hall he said, "Listen, Red, I'm sure the President must think, because of all the noise Anne made up in Connecticut, that I was a Nixon man all the way. I was not. She just got so wound up and involved it looked as though I was just as committed. That wasn't the case. To support her, I gave five thousand dollars to the Nixon campaign and then I gave five thousand dollars to Jack's campaign. But more important, I'm a patriotic American. I want to help and I think I can make a contribution. I'd like to serve in some sort of a role if I could . . . in some capacity."

"Let me talk to the President," I said.

Then we started talking about Bob McNamara.

"It's too bad for you, losing such an outstanding man, but it was a very generous, patriotic contribution on your part to let him go," I said.

"What do you mean 'let him'?" he said. "I didn't even know about Bob McNamara's being offered a job until a friend of mine happened to mention that he'd heard that an offer had been made. Nobody came to me and asked me what I wanted. I got it all secondhand. I was disturbed about it. At least I should have been informed that he was going to be approached."

"I'm sure it was an oversight of some kind," I said. "There was so much going on at that time that somebody must have thought that somebody else had made the contact, and it was just something that fell through the cracks." And I added: "What a great sacrifice it is for Bob McNamara financially."

"I wouldn't worry about Bob McNamara financially," Henry said. "We paid him pretty well at Ford Motor Company. He's gotta be a pretty wealthy man today."

Henry told me that Bob McNamara had been of tremendous service to the company and had made a lasting contribution. "Through his methods and procedures, we became much more responsive to changes. Now when we sense a change in the public's buying desires we can be immediately responsive instead of having to wait as much as three years." Then he added: "But, Red, Bob McNamara doesn't have everything— he needs a little bit of your warmth and humor. Boy, that guy is a real cold drink of water."

Henry's analysis of Bob McNamara's personality wasn't very far off the mark. If there is a weakness in our great Secretary of Defense, it is his inability to get along well with people who do not share his opinions and positions. Many Senators and Congressmen can show bruises and abrasions they've received in exchanges with McNamara.

Later on I told the President of Henry's desire to serve. With an underlying friendliness toward the head of the Ford Motor Company, he replied, "Well, we'll see if we can't find a spot for good old Henry."

I never did follow up to see if Henry was offered anything.

CHAPTER TWENTY

HROUGHOUT HIS POLITICAL career, John Kennedy displayed an extraordinary understanding of the way his words and actions, and the words and behavior of those around him, would appear to other people.

In one of my expansive moments before my governmental career began, I bought a red sport jacket. I brought it along with me to Washington, and made the mistake of wearing it to an informal party which the President attended.

With that very special touch which made you feel he cared but also let you know that a change was required, he said, "Look, we'll hang up the red coat for the duration. We're trying to create a responsible image of the New Frontier, as well as projecting Red Fay as a serious-minded administrator and not just Grand Old Lovable."

The red coat resided in the closet for the duration.

One day my shirts came under scrutiny. He said to me, "Where did you get that shirt? Look at the collar on that thing. It goes out too wide and it's too long. What you ought to wear is one of these nice, short-pointed collars."

As he rubbed his own shirt, he added: "The button-down collars are too Ivy League and collegiate. Those other shirts you've been wearing have collars that are too long. Take a look at this. Why don't you let me order some for you from my shirtmaker in New York?"

Being rather close with a buck, I inquired, "What would they run apiece?"

"Probably twenty or twenty-five dollars."

"Mr. President," I said, "When I'm your Vice President then I will start moving into the twenty-five-dollars-per-shirt class."

While he appreciated good-looking shirts, ties, suits and jackets, he decided early in life that he did not look well in a hat. He recognized that a hat belonged in the well-dressed man's wardrobe, but he would only go so far as to carry one in his hand.

When he became President, this personal aversion took on far greater significance. The hat industry was suffering because of the President's reluctance to wear a hat.

Nice Al Webb, who was the Eastern representative for one of the major hat manufacturers, was considered their only possible savior because of his friendship with the President.

"We're dying in the business without you wearing a hat,"

Al told the President. "Can't you put one on now and then?"

The President appreciated the serious effect his refusal to wear a hat had on the industry, as well as the great strain on Nice Al.

"Al," he'd reply, "I've tried wearing hats and I'm just not the type. When I get one on I feel like I'm wearing a tent. Look, I'll carry a hat for you. How would that be?"

Poor Nice Al gave a weak smile of acceptance.

I personally thought the President looked great in a hat. "To be completely honest, and not just to help good old Al, I think you look damn well in a hat," I told him.

All these arguments were to no avail. But in a last attempt, Al said, "Mr. President, let me make up a hat for you. I know exactly the style you ought to wear. I'll bring it down next week and you can see for yourself."

The week passed and Nice Al came down with two hats, one for me and one for the President. I was seated in my office in the Pentagon when the phone buzzed.

"Red," the President said, "Nice Al is down with the hats. I told him he could bring them over at 5:30 P.M. Come over so we can satisfy Al once and for all."

At 5:30 we all gathered in the President's office for our hat-trying. Al was carrying the weight of the hat industry on his shoulders. If the President continued to refuse to wear a hat, the hat business would undoubtedly suffer.

Al took the hats out of their boxes as if he was handling a couple of Stradivariuses. The President and I tried them on. Standing off like the master viewing his greatest work, Al said, "You both look great."

The President and I looked at each other and burst out laughing.

"Al," the President said, "are you willing to destroy the beloved image of our country's leader just to save the hat industry?"

The President called for a photographer to preserve a permanent record of the hour the final decision was made that John F. Kennedy, thirty-fifth President of the U.S.A., would not wear a hat.

The question of whether or not to wear a hat was easily resolved, but the President faced more of a problem with two other matters: rumors about his health and about a supposed earlier marriage.

In August or September, 1963, he was having trouble with his groin. He had pulled a muscle, perhaps as an indirect result of his problems with his back. He found the physical limitations from the injury a nuisance, but he was more concerned about projecting an image that he was slowly disintegrating.

"Now listen, Pierre," he said to Salinger, "I don't want to read anything in the papers about my groin. We can attribute it all to the back. If I'm not playing golf, I'm still having trouble with my back. I don't want the American public thinking that their President is falling apart: 'Now he's got a bad back, now his groin is going.' The next thing the Republicans will be claiming, 'Now it's his brain.' "

The rumors of a "secret marriage" presented more of a problem, but the President was less disturbed by that irresponsible gossip than I was. I was at a dinner party in Pasadena when I first heard the charge that Jack had married Durie Shevlin before his marriage to Jacqueline.

My informants refused to tell me the source of this rumor.

211

They seemed to imply that any such revelation would be a gross breach of honor, but they had no hesitation in casting doubt on the character of the President of the United States.

After that first exposure to this nonsense, I began hearing similar reports at many gatherings. Finally I spoke to the President about it.

"I don't understand why you don't make a statement at one of your press conferences revealing the falseness of the whole story. I can't go to a dinner or a cocktail party outside of this town without some righteous woman informing me of what I should know about my President."

Resigned and unconcerned, Jack said, "Red, if I make a statement to the public on everything I have been accused of, I'd spend all my time on radio and television trying to keep the record straight. If people want to believe such tales, no denial on my part is going to convince them differently."

Finally *Newsweek* magazine, published by the President's friend, Philip Graham, exposed the rumor and the rumor-mongers for what they were—namely, carriers of lies and slander.

Bob Kennedy was particularly sensitive about another public relations problem for the New Frontier—the use of U.S. Government automobiles and Government-paid drivers. He didn't want the taxpayers to get the impression that they were supporting a lot of political appointees who were expanding beyond their intended use such unaccustomed luxuries as chauffeured cars.

Nothing on occasion seemed to disturb Bob more than to see my wife drive up in my official black sedan, even if she were coming by to pick up Ethel to take her to some political or military reception. On the few occasions when we didn't take our own private car when we went over to the Kennedys' for dinner, we'd have our official driver, Oliver Washington, park in the back or off to one side so Bob wouldn't see him. This wasn't out of a sense of guilt, but was just a precaution to make the evening at the Kennedys' that much more enjoyable.

One night we told Washington to park down the road behind other cars so I wouldn't have to go through a detailed explanation to the Attorney General on why we were in the government car.

When we were ready to leave, Bob walked us to the door and out into the cold air at the front door. Any minute I expected those hawk eyes to pick out my sedan, and I was ready for the tirade to begin. Fortunately, Bob didn't see the car, so no explanations were necessary.

When my wife and I reached the car, there was no Washington. I spotted one of the Kennedys' drivers and asked if he knew where Washington was.

"Yes, he is in the kitchen, talking to Ruby," the driver said. (Ruby was the cook and one fine gal.) "I'll call him."

He disappeared for a few minutes. Then we noticed Bob at the front door landing, bidding good night to more of his guests.

At the same moment, Washington came out the back door, hurrying but trying to be as inconspicuous as possible. Out of nowhere came Megin, the mean old Kennedy Saint Bernard, barking as though he were on the trail of an escaping convict. Across the lawn right in front of Bob Kennedy, with Megin hot on his heels, flashed Washington, running at top speed.

213

I figured the case was lost, that in seconds Bob would be down there rasping, "What right have you to be here with a Government car and driver?" But Washington made it into the safety of the car in seconds, just as Megin made his last unfulfilled leap at the door. We were out on the country road quickly, having escaped a confrontation.

A few days later, Bob asked me, "Did you see someone streak across the lawn the other night just as you left? We never found out who it was. Did you recognize him?"

With complete loss of integrity, I responded, "Never even saw him."

Early in his Presidency, a committee of PT boat veterans came to Washington to present a Steuben glass memento of the insignia of his PT boat under the Presidential seal to the President. He gave a reception for the men and their wives, and I took the liberty of asking Jack Warnecke, an old pal of mine, to come to the reception. The President knew Warnecke only casually, but as we walked into the room where the reception was being held, he spotted Warnecke at once.

"Rosebowl," the President said, using the nickname Warnecke had acquired as the result of his spectacular performance in the Rose Bowl, "what are you doing here? You were never in PT's."

I came to the rescue. Since Warnecke was with Jane Wheeler, I said to the President, "We had to get an acceptable escort for Jane."

The President and Warnecke chatted for a few minutes, and the next night at dinner he asked me, "What does Rosebowl do?"

"He's a very successful architect, and is back here now for some high-level AIA meeting," I said.

After a moment's thought, the President said, "Have him call me tomorrow morning at 9:30. Jackie is very upset about the plans for the new building to be put up around Lafayette Square. She feels that what they are planning will ruin the beauty and the historic charm of this area, and I agree with her."

The next day, Rosebowl called the President, and was told of the President's apprehensions about the square. That weekend he spent hours walking around the square to absorb the President's own feeling about it, and even located a relief of the square which he studied thoroughly. He made photographs of the area from different angles, and on Monday morning in the Cabinet Room he offered his plans to the President and Jacqueline. Both were enthusiastic and approved his concept. Today, a large new building fits naturally and attractively into the area without spoiling the general appearance and the charm of the old buildings that surround the square.

CHAPTER TWENTY-ONE

JOHN KENNEDY WAS always somewhat amazed and intrigued by the life of his predecessor, General Dwight D. Eisenhower. One day, we flew over Ike's Gettysburg farm when we were visiting the battlefields at Gettysburg. Looking down at the beautiful farmhouse, the spacious metal barns, quantities of farm equipment, the freshly painted fence and an assortment of thoroughbred stock, Jack said with a trace of wonder plus curiosity, "There doesn't seem to be too strong a basis for a military pay raise if Ike could accumulate all this spread starting as a second looey."

He did not begrudge Ike any of his material possessions. In

fact, he respected Ike, but he was fascinated by the demands of a military career.

Opening the topic into a broader field, he continued, "The demanding promotion course has its advantages and disadvantages. Certainly it rewards the industrious, bright, ambitious officer, but only so long as he conforms to the pattern of the Establishment. You have to kowtow to the admirals and generals all the way up, and your own wife has to put up with the admiral's wife who might be the worst old bag on the station. If you express a position in opposition to that of your commanding officer, who might be very unimaginative, even though you are confident it is a much better approach to the problem at hand, you're playing with dynamite. Number one, it is unmilitary; and number two, by the nature of the promotion system senior officers will most likely be in a position to stick it into you for years to come. So what happens? You end up with hard-working, honest, industrious men ready to fight but notoriously lacking in original thought as compared to their counterparts in civilian life."

While he had developed an extremely critical attitude toward some top officers, the President never lost his close identification with the other members of the armed services, particularly those of the Navy. He looked back on his own days in the Navy with the same nostalgia an outstanding football player often feels about his college years.

One day in the Cabinet Room of the White House, a Marine crew was filming the prologue to *The John Glenn Story*. They were operating under the direction of my Marine aide, Colonel Jim Stockman, and seemed to have enough equipment to film *Gone With the Wind*.

The crew was to photograph the President that morning, and Jim and I had worked out a brief script for him. We placed it on the Cabinet table in front of the President's seat.

When he entered, every Marine, without waiting for an order, snapped to attention. Jack couldn't conceal his obvious admiration for their bearing.

I introduced Colonel Stockman, who in turn introduced the chief warrant officer in charge of the Marine camera crew. Slightly self-conscious because of the wide gap between an informal civilian introduction and the immobility of the men at attention, the President nodded acknowledgment. Then he asked, "Is this the script?"

"Yes, Mr. President," I said.

He swept through the two or three pages. Reaching for a pencil, he deleted a few parts and scribbled in some minor changes.

"All right, let's go ahead," he said. Looking around, he asked, "Who is in charge here?"

Stockman responded, "Chief Warrant Officer ———."

"All right, Chief," the President said, "you're in charge now."

The chief warrant officer took him at his word. Within seconds, he was barking out commands at the President, who obviously was amused. When the filming was completed, the President said, "Chief, I'm not sure whether I could have made it through recruit training if you had been my drill sergeant."

"I'm sure you would have, Sir," the CWO said, without batting an eye.

Still smiling, the President said, "Thanks, Chief."

The President stopped for a brief moment to speak to Jim before leaving.

"Colonel," he said, "where did you get your Silver Star?"

"At Okinawa, Mr. President," Jim said.

Without hesitating, the President continued, "Were you with the 1st or the 3rd Marine Division?"

"The 1st, Mr. President."

"Colonel, you were part of the world's best," the President said as he took his leave.

His intimate knowledge of military units and military history was a labor of love. He also had a strong interest in the educational and physical fitness programs of the services.

"What is lacking in the education of a naval officer that appears to be fulfilled in the education of an Army officer?" he once asked me. "Look through our history. What naval officers have gone on after their naval careers to serve with as much distinction in other assignments as the men the Army has provided?"

Before I could answer, he said, "The Army has given us Eisenhower, MacArthur, Maxwell Taylor, Lucius Clay, George Marshall."

Then he mused, "It might not be a bad idea to have the same test given to all the academies in fields of similar study to see how they compared. From what I have been able to find out, it's very possible that the Coast Guard Academy graduates would stand the highest."

Knowing of his love of the sea and his strong attachment to the armed forces, the Navy and Marine Corps arranged for maneuvers in April, 1962, to display for the President the readiness of the modern fleet to meet any challenge. There were some great moments during the maneuvers staged off the East Coast, but there were some other moments that resulted in justifiably strong criticism from the President.

The President and many members of Congress and most of

the diplomatic corps were there to witness the maneuvers. He wanted them to enjoy their hours on the U.S.S. *Northampton,* and therefore sent word to the Secretary of the Navy that he would like arrangements made to serve cocktails aboard ship before dinner.

When word of this request reached the Navy, Fred Korth, then Secretary of the Navy, started desperately reaching for ways and means to satisfy the President's request. From every man in blue who was queried came the same reply: "Liquor hasn't been served aboard a Navy ship since the days of Josephus Daniels. It's against Navy regulations."

"I don't give a damn about Navy regulations," Secretary Fred Korth responded, but the undercurrent of opposition was so strong that I wondered whether a simple order carrying out the President's wishes would actually leave the Secretary's office. Word must have filtered over to the White House about this minor crisis in the Pentagon, because a message soon reached us which offered a simple solution: "While the President of the United States is aboard the *Northampton,* the ward room, his quarters, and such areas as he designates will be considered as the White House."

Before boarding the *Northampton* on the evening of April 13, the President inspected the *Thomas A. Edison,* a nuclear submarine. When he reached the pier where the sub was docked, a raw, icy wind was sweeping in off the Atlantic. Because he was then suffering from his back injuries, a makeshift elevator was used to lower him into the *Thomas A. Edison.*

The captain guided him around the sub, explaining the exceptionally complicated and sophisticated systems provided

220

to assure accurate navigation and missile firing. The President was fascinated by the systems, and fell behind schedule.

He did not know that a group of underwater swimmers was standing in the icy, biting wind on the pier awaiting inspection. As soon as he came up from the submarine, the President made his review of the shivering men as swiftly as possible, but still found a word or two for each of them.

Coming upon a sailor in swimming trunks who was shaking all over from the cold, the President said, "The Admiral here tells me you fellows don't even feel the cold." The sailor couldn't help laughing. The President continued, "Well, we're getting right out of here and you fellows can get in out of the cold and warm up."

"Mr. President," the sailor answered without hesitation, "I'd be happy to stand out here in the cold indefinitely to meet you."

The President smiled and patted the sailor's icy shoulder. "Thanks, but if you don't get out of this cold pretty soon we'll never meet again."

The next stop was the *Northampton*. I reached the ship shortly after the President had boarded her, and immediately received word that the President wanted to see me in his stateroom. As my assigned quarters were only two doors away on the same deck, I was in his stateroom almost upon receiving the orders. I found him doing his calisthenics, working mostly on his stomach and back muscles.

He was still elated over the news that the steel companies had rescinded their price increase that afternoon. When he felt that way, it affected everyone around him. His smile was quicker, his appreciation broader, his humor continuous.

"If any one person deserves the credit for having the steel

companies see the light," he said, "it has to be Clark Clifford. Since he represents so many of them here in Washington, he had immediate entree. Can't you just see Clifford outlining the possible courses of action the government could take if they showed signs of not moving?"

Then, as if purging his mind of any deviation from accepted social practices, he said with feeling, "What matters is that the price line was held. Now it will be easier to deal with the unions on their round of bargaining. This will help prevent inflation, and the country should continue to enjoy prosperity."

Dave Powers, Kenny O'Donnell, Ben Smith and Larry O'Brien had all congregated in the outer stateroom for a drink before going below. When the President came out to join them, everyone sensed his delight over the steel price rollback. After several toasts, Dave Powers, a great baseball authority, shouted, "The Babe has been at the plate and just hit that Big Steel pitcher for a home run. Let's do the job right and knock him right out of the box."

Dave had no chance to complete his analogy. Sensing the "Hit him again while he's down" feeling in the atmosphere, the President cut in.

"Let's all understand one thing and never be quoted to the contrary," he said. "Steel rescinded their price increases and we are pleased. But now it has been done and we want to give them every bit of help we can. If they don't prosper, the whole economy is in trouble." The conversation turned to other topics.

The next morning the maneuvers started. The entire fleet passed in review before the President, led by the mighty nuclear-powered carrier, the *Enterprise*. We were then transported by helicopter to the *Enterprise* itself. The fleet divided into two long lines of ships, one led by the *Enterprise* and the other by the *Forrestal*.

To grasp the magnitude of the maneuvers, I climbed up near the top of the mainmast, just below the radar. Almost as far back as I could see, the ships of the fleet were strung out, their bows plunging through the choppy seas, sending out ever-diminishing waves angling off into the water.

The exercise started with an antisubmarine attack, with fixed-wing aircraft dropping bombs and depth charges. Helicopters with dipping sonars traced the evasive tactics of the submarine.

When the submarine surfaced, signaling the end of the anti-sub warfare exercise, the air-to-air missile exercise began. Sidewinders, which are designed to zero in on heat such as the exhaust of a jet, were to be used.

A pair of jets zoomed down between the two lines of ships, about a hundred feet off the water. When they were just astern, they started to climb, releasing glowing flares as targets for the Sidewinder missiles.

Soon the missile-laden Phantom jet fighters followed, flying at about the speed of sound. When the Phantoms were abreast of the *Enterprise,* they fired their missiles. The Sidewinders shot out, each with a vapor trail behind it. Everyone watched, transfixed, awaiting the frantic rush of the missile toward its glowing target.

Then the seemingly impossible occurred. Both missiles started to run erratic courses and eventually fell into the sea. More Phantoms fired at a second set of flares. This time one Sidewinder faltered, but the other found its target. The assembled crowd let out a cheer, more in relief than in admiration.

Soon after that near-fiasco, the surface-to-air missile demonstration began. Above us in the clear blue sky at about ten thousand feet a radio-controlled obsolete 9F9 fighter, serving as a drone, could be seen flying straight and true in the direction of the fleet. Being relatively high, it appeared to be moving slowly, holding its altitude.

The loudspeaker system barked: "Missiles ready to fire." Seconds later, first one and then another missile streaked skyward from the ship astern. After a few more seconds, first one and then the other missile started to run erratically. The target plane flew serenely on, uninterrupted, directly over the entire fleet.

The exercises for the day had been concluded no more than two or three minutes when a young naval officer came rushing up to me with a look of considerable alarm on his face. Almost out of breath, he said, "Mr. Secretary, the President would like you to join him for lunch in his quarters. If you will follow me, I'll take you there."

The President had the stateroom and suite generally set aside for the fleet admiral. When I walked in, the same men who had been with us just before dinner on the *Northampton* the night before were there. Dave Powers spotted me first. In that happy, lyrical voice he called, "Here he is now, Mr. President, the man who planned it all." Dave and the others there knew that I had just about as much to do with the whole operation as they did. In spite of Dave's attempt to add a touch of levity, I could see that the President was not amused.

"My God," he said. "Based on the success of the operations I've seen today, I'm sure the word has already gotten to Moscow, 'Come in by sea.' "

Then, speaking in a lower tone and more concerned voice,

he continued: "What irritated me was the seemingly self-satisfied air of some of your admirals who looked as if nothing had happened. Six missiles are fired and one hits its target, and that target was hardly moving. There were diplomats from almost every country on the globe watching those failures. I'd asked them out to witness the might of the United States, to make them a little bit more willing to embrace our policies when they were being pressured to the contrary. What happens? Under ideal conditions, all prearranged with no outside harassment, we have an 80 percent failure. My God, if I were going to ask the President of the United States and all the top members of the diplomatic corps to watch a surface-to-air missile shoot, I damn well would be ready to fire more than two missiles. And if it looked like I wasn't going to get a hit out of four or six of them, I'd make damn sure that plane exploded if the last missile even came near it."

He was absolutely right. If we hadn't felt reasonably sure of success, it was folly to prepare such a gigantic production and come up with only a peep. Fortunately, the Marines put on a fantastic performance that afternoon, so the final impression left at the end of the two-day operation was one of power and precision.

Before we left the *Enterprise,* Kenny O'Donnell told me a story about a supposed meeting between the President and an ambassador from one of the major Latin-American countries.

"Mr. Ambassador," the President said, "we were delighted to have you out here today to witness these maneuvers. We want you to know if you would like to buy some surface-to-air missiles, or the whole missile system, we would be delighted to enter into negotiations with your people."

The ambassador replied in rather an apologetic tone. "Oh,

225

Mr. President, you are so kind to offer us this wonderful missile and the missile system. I know that it would be very good for our Navy to own them. But if you don't mind, instead could you sell us some of those drones?" describing them by slowly moving his hand high in an arc over his head.

The President had just finished his remarks about the missile demonstration when lunch came in. He was still obviously disturbed by the morning's failures, and seemed edgy and fidgety.

He tasted the soup.

"It's cold," he said, pushing it aside after taking one hurried spoonful. "Where is the rest of the meal?"

A very shy Filipino steward came forward with a platter of fried chicken and served the President. As the first piece of chicken touched his mouth, the President said, with considerable irritation, "My God, this is fried chicken! Where is the chief?"

The chief steward came forward to take the fire. You could almost see him bracing himself.

"Chief, I gave orders around here that I can't eat fried foods. This is fried chicken. You have two choices. You can broil chicken or you can fry it. My request was that you *broil* it. And what do I get? Fried chicken. I don't think I was asking too much."

Then, feeling perhaps that he had made too much of the incident or was taking out on the chief the problems of the day, the President's face suddenly softened, and his tone changed. With a slight smile at the corners of his mouth, he said to the chief, "Chief, don't ever let those gunner's mates ever tell you that they are the only ones with hardship duty."

Knowing he had been forgiven, the chief smiled. "It won't happen again, Mr. President," he said.

A little more than a year later, the Navy staged Presidential maneuvers off the West Coast. Upon arriving, the President and his party were led out upon the flight deck of the *Kitty Hawk,* just forward of the "island." A row of seats had been set up, facing forward and to starboard, and from there the Presidential party was to observe fly-bys, missile shoots, and other maneuvers.

Directly up the flight deck from us, perhaps twenty yards away, were about thirty photographers and correspondents. The photographers were shooting picture after picture, as though they expected at any moment to be ordered below.

The President was flanked on his left by Secretary of the Navy Korth, Chief of Naval Operations Admiral George Anderson, and so on down the line of authority. On his right were Governor Pat Brown of California, Senator Clair Engle, then myself, and on my right the Commandant of the Marine Corps, General Dave Shoup.

About midway through the maneuvers a bevy of stewards began serving coffee. They served the President first, then fanned out in both directions. The coffee steward came first, then another with cream and sugar.

The President, having already received his coffee, sugar and cream, turned to speak to Pat Brown just as the Governor was being offered cream. Pat tried to give the President his full attention while taking the cream at the same time. As a result, he put his forefinger into the pitcher, and pulled the cream over into his lap. Startled, he jumped to his feet. But

227

then he realized that the eyes of the correspondents and photographers were focused on him, and sat down again. The cream that had not adhered to his trousers had formed a pool in his chair, and as soon as the Governor felt that unexpected second wave of cream he shot to his feet again.

The President had managed to hold back during the first part of the sequence, but by this time the whole situation was so ludicrous that he burst into laughter. While the Governor tried to remove the remaining cream from the front of his trousers, Senator Engle reached over with a napkin and began blotting the Governor's rear. Leaning over me, General Shoup, a Congressional Medal of Honor winner and a Marine's Marine, said, "You might have kissed his ——— before, but I'll bet you never thought you'd get around to ——— it, too."

When the crisis was finally brought under control, the President leaned over to the Governor. "Pat," he whispered, "with that phalanx of photographers in front of me, that steward could have poured boiling oil onto my lap and I still would have smiled."

In the ride down from the China Lake Facility where weapons of the future were tested for the President, Governor Pat Brown, Senator Clair Engle and I sat with the President in the forward compartment of the helicopter. Our talk dealt almost solely with California, its problems and assets. I was extremely impressed with the Governor's keen knowledge of all the issues discussed, even down to small facts and figures. The conversation eventually turned to the Chessman case.

As Pat told of his agonizing experiences during that period, you couldn't help but recognize the almost beguiling charm that had made him such a successful political figure. There was a quality of frankness, near-naïveté and complete honesty not ordinarily found in a markedly successful politician, as Pat must be credited with being.

Describing the booing and hooting he received almost wherever he went during that period, he stated, "It got so bad that I didn't want to go out where I would be seen in public. I worried about the effect it would have on my family. Imagine a politician trying every way he could to avoid making speeches. Well, that is what that Chessman episode did to me."

That night, when we had a chance to recall many of the incidents of the day, the President said in an almost incredulous tone, "That Pat Brown is something. Have you ever known anyone so high in public life who speaks out his innermost feeling with such complete frankness? Here he is, Governor of probably the most powerful state in the Union, and he treats everyone as though they are doing him a favor being nice to him."

When we hit the beach that evening, there on the front page of every paper was the photograph of the cream-spilling episode, with the startled Pat next to the President, who was unsuccessfully trying to suppress his laughter. The President asked Kenny O'Donnell to get him an enlarged copy. When it came, the President presented it to Pat with the inscription, "It only hurts when you laugh."

After the maneuvers, the President was to be guest of honor at a Democratic fund-raising party at the Beverly Hills Hotel.

The dinner was originally scheduled for a ballroom where a local high school traditionally held its senior prom. The Democrats had pre-empted the ballroom briefly, and one of the students had written the President a very polite letter explaining the problem.

Incensed by the arbitrary action of the dinner planners, the

President gave positive instructions that the room be immediately turned back to the high school seniors. Arrangements could be made for the fund-raising dinner in a different room, he said. As it worked out, the dinner was a much greater success. Instead of the usual one-hundred-dollar-per-plate dinner, the ante was raised to a thousand dollars, which attracted a smaller but more intimate—and more generous—gathering.

There were about twenty tables of ten people each. The President visited each table for from seven to ten minutes. This was the first time most of the donors had ever been close to the President, and they were very pleased to have this chance to sit and chat with him.

About eleven o'clock, the President indicated he wanted to go downstairs to thank the high school group for their courteous request to him and to talk very briefly to them. Pat said to several of us, "I think it would be nice if I went down ahead and told the students that the President is going to come down and visit them, and also how proud I am as their Governor of how they conducted themselves. What do you think?"

All of us told him it seemed like a great idea, and a few minutes later Pat went down. He came back in about a half-hour, commenting, "What nice kids. They are terribly excited about the President's visit."

When the President went down later to speak to the students, I was detained at the dinner and missed his talk. About midnight, I went down to get a newspaper, and ran into one of the members of the White House entourage, who seemed somewhat worked up.

"Mr. Secretary," he said, "I don't know whether you can

do anything about it, but the Governor came into one of the ballrooms and told the students there that the President was going to come down and talk to them. The President hasn't come, and from what reports I get no one is making any moves to get him to come."

I was baffled, because I knew the President had intended to speak to the students earlier and to the best of my knowledge had left the dinner party to do just that.

"I'll check up on it, but I thought the President had already visited the students," I said. I phoned upstairs to the Presidential suite and got Dave Powers on the line, and explained the predicament. Dave turned to question the President, who immediately came on the line.

"Listen, I've already spoken to those high school students," he said.

"That's what I told them down here, but they say you haven't and the Governor said you were going to," I said.

The President paused a moment and then said, "Which high school prom are you talking about?"

I gave him the name of the school.

The President laughed. Obviously turning to Kenny, he said, "Pat went downstairs and spoke to the wrong high school." Then, coming back to the phone, he continued, "You heard what I said. Listen, I can't come down to speak to every high school group in the hotel. The next thing you know I'll be asked to speak at grammar school gatherings with maybe a few words for the kindergarten group. I'll send Peter down. He owes something to that age group."

Peter Lawford saved the day, and might have been just what that age group wanted.

CHAPTER TWENTY-TWO

O FTEN ON SATURDAY mornings up at the Cape, I would hear that famous voice calling, "John, time to go for a drive," or "Miss Shaw, it's time for Father and Son to get to know each other. Where is that boy?"

After John, Jr. had been found, there was almost always a personality struggle to determine who was going to give orders, John or his father.

"John, you sit right here next to your father," the President would say, indicating a spot on the front seat.

John would invariably sit as far over on the other side as he could, relishing the game with his father. But after a few

232

minutes the game would end and he would be up standing next to his dad, with his left arm around his father's neck and the other pointing out the wonder of the moment. Behind us would be two or three cars filled with Secret Service men.

Down at the toy store, where the staff soon became accustomed to the Presidential visits, John was in a world of his own. Oblivious of anyone around, he was soon down on the floor, carefully studying the particular toy his father had handed him. He might turn his head briefly if you held up another toy and spoke to him about it, but his attention could rarely be diverted from the toy he had before him.

When the time came to make a purchase, it was a most informal commercial transaction. The President would say simply, "We'll take these. Put them on the bill." And out we would go. John would lead the pack, jumping, skipping or running to get into the car.

John, Jr.'s totally uninhibited personality delighted his father. The President couldn't keep his hands off his son. When they were together the President was always taunting and teasing him, and watching with great pleasure John's youthful responses. I felt that the father realized more vividly than most of us that the process of growing up would soon bring to an end the wonderful honest charm of a boy discovering the world around him.

John teased the President almost as much as the President teased him. If he knew his father was trying to catch him, he would run, bubbling with laughter. If caught, he would struggle, argue and complain, "Daddy, let me go. You let me go. Mommy, make Daddy let me go."

When he was released, the game would start all over again,

generally ending when Mommy said, "Time for dinner," or when some other childhood appointment had to be met. Off he would go, his hand in Maud Shaw's, chattering away, probably about how he fooled Daddy.

One weekend, Anita, Sally and I came up with the President on a Friday afternoon. As soon as we disembarked from Air Force One at the Air Force base just outside of Hyannis Port, we saw Jacqueline, John and Caroline.

Spotting his dad coming down the ramp, John took off in full flight in his direction. The next day the papers carried a picture of John in full stride, one toe barely touching the ground and the other back up behind him as high as his head as he was rushing forward, to be caught in his father's arms.

Walter Pidgeon sent the President a clipping with a quotation: "An unbound spirit, whose race has just begun . . ."

Jack saw the picture and said with a smile, "Every mother in the United States is saying, 'Isn't it wonderful to see that love between a son and his father, the way that John races to be with his father?' Little do they know that that son would have raced right by his father to get to that helicopter but his dad stepped into his path and grabbed him."

This incident took place just the weekend before Patrick Bouvier Kennedy was born. Jack spoke to me only once about the loss of his second son, but those few words revealed his grief.

"It is so hard for Jackie," he said. "She wanted so to have another child. Then after all the difficulties she has in bearing a child, to lose him is doubly hard." Wistfully, his words trailing off as though he were seeing the years ahead, he added: "It has been so much fun with 'Buttons' and John, it would have been nice to have another son."

I'm sure in the loneliness of his thoughts he often relived the agony of that loss, but he never again spoke to me of Patrick's death, and this was characteristic. He did not brood over the tragedies that were beyond his power to change.

He accepted the idea of sorrow and death. When his friends think of him, they recall the occasional moments when the depths of his feelings were revealed suddenly but briefly. But John Kennedy was a happy man, and those who knew him well will always remember him that way.

I recall the Saturday before Easter in 1963. About ten o'clock that morning, the President decided to take my daughter, Sally, Caroline and John downtown on a toy-shopping spree.

"Come on, you lucky children," he called. "Your wonderful dads are taking you downtown to explore the wonders of the toy stores."

With two cars filled with Secret Service men following discreetly about two car lengths behind us, the President drove the Mercury convertible down to one of the Palm Beach shopping centers.

The minute we entered a large toy store, I could sense the excitement caused by the President's presence. But almost everyone in the store respected the President's right to privacy. A few children and two adults did ask shyly for his autograph. Between these infrequent intrusions, Jack would throw himself zestfully into the task of buying presents for his children.

When I saw how enthusiastic he was, I eased over toward him and in a muffled tone said, "Mr. President, let's not go too strong on toys. If you go for a couple of fifty-dollar purchases, Old Dad here is going to have to come someplace close to that or look like a real nickel-nose to his darling Sal."

All I got in return was a wide-eyed look, with a trace of a smile which meant: "Redhead, what a wonderful day this is going to be for Sal." Then, as if repenting, he said, "Everything will be held within modest restraint."

John then spotted a stuffed dog about the size of a Saint Bernard. Chattering, skipping and jumping, he hugged the dog.

Jack leaned over to the salesman and inquired in a whisper, "How much is the dog?" The price was something over a hundred dollars. The shocked look on Jack's face assured me that the toy budget wasn't going to be stretched that far. With a certain sadistic pleasure, I said to the President's son, "John, I really think that dog loves you already."

The President, sensing a possible fleecing ahead, immediately said in an authoritative tone, "John, there will be no dog today. The gentleman has a very special helicopter for you."

In a matter of seconds John was completely engrossed in the helicopter.

When we finally cleared the toy store the President was about forty dollars lighter and I was about twelve dollars lighter. I felt I had escaped with a minimum of damage.

We then went down to Lilly Pulitzer's shop in the central shopping area on Worth Avenue. As soon as we entered the store, people started pouring in. In seconds it was so jammed that Lilly ordered the doors closed. Jack bought dresses for Jacqueline and Caroline, and then came over to help me pick out dresses for my wife, Sally and Kathy. He'd say, "Now, Red, here is one for the Bride, and these would look good on Kathy

236

or Sally." I felt a certain reassurance about the soundness of my purchases after they had been approved by the President of the United States.

When we were ready to leave, Lilly said, "Why don't you go out the back door so you can avoid the crowd waiting outside?" We followed her advice, and found ourselves in a little inner court, facing the back entrances to some of the other shops in the area. We started to go through a little arcade to the main street, but stopped when we saw the crowd still waiting in front of Lilly's.

To escape the growing mob, we scurried from back door to back door. Amused by our predicament, the President said, "I'm awfully glad this whole episode is not on television. There is something about it which doesn't quite befit the role of the President."

In our search for an avenue of escape, we ran into the kitchen of a restaurant. The look of surprise on the faces of the cooks reminded me of scenes from old movie farces. Next we started into a women's clothing store. The President asked a woman who appeared to be the owner, "Would it be all right if we pass through your store?"

"It is perfectly all right if you walk slowly going out the front door," she said with a touch of humor. "I want everybody on Worth Avenue to see you coming out of my store."

Having evaded the crowd, we walked across the street and into Schur's. Obviously this was not John Kennedy's first visit to the shop, as he was greeted as an old friend.

"Let's take a look at some of those sport shirts," the President said and pointed to a display table stacked high with shirts. The colors that he preferred were beige, rust and olive green. Picking out a few, he turned to me and said, "These ought to look good on you." He held up two shirts—one navy blue and the other olive green. Then he said, "I'm going to buy you a pair of slacks and a sport shirt. It will be my personal contribution to the campaign to clean up Red Fay."

"John," he said to the owner, "do you think it is possible to make a style leader out of the Under Secretary? See if you can outfit him with a pair of those raspberry-colored slacks."

John was not about to lose the sale. I was outfitted in a pair of slacks that I will treasure all my life.

During that visit to Palm Beach, John, Jr. picked up a new description to use in teasing his father—Foo-Foo Head. Where John got the name or what it means only a child would know.

We were swimming in the pool the morning John first experimented with the new expression. He was in his inflated swimming ring, splashing, laughing, talking and teasing his father.

Jack tried to divide his attention equally between his children, but since Caroline had my daughter, Sally, as a companion during our visit, the bubbling, uninhibited, bouncy John was generally center stage front.

It was a running contest between father and son. John would splash his dad or, with excitement creeping into his eyes, say, "Silly Daddy." Having achieved a major triumph, he would paddle gleefully and furiously away to escape his pursuing father.

Some time during this exchange, John determined he was going to get out of the pool and started up the concrete stairs. No sooner had that firm little rump cleared the water than the President pulled John's trunks down below his buttocks, pulling him back into the water.

John, squalling in indignation, scolded his father, "Naughty Daddy," and started back up again. This little episode was repeated several times until John finally made it to the safety of the walk that surrounded the pool.

Once John was beyond the reach of his father's arm, the glint of daring was back in his eyes. Leaning toward the pool, well out of reach of his father, John called, "Daddy, you are a Foo-Foo Head."

Then, estimating that he had scored the winning thrust, he turned and bounded away, giggling as his father in mock disapproval called, "John Kennedy, how dare you call the President of the United States a Foo-Foo Head? You rascal, you wait till I get ahold of you."

There were several more calls of "Daddy, you are a Foo-Foo Head," with just the right response from his dad.

That evening the former Ambassador to Cuba, Earl Smith, and his wife Flo came for dinner. While seven of us were just finishing our first course, the children came in to say good night before going to bed. Around the table they went, John kissing the ladies and bowing to the men as he shook hands.

When they had completed their good nights and were leaving the patio, he turned around with a mischievous look in his eye. Waiting a few seconds till he caught his father's eye, he leaned slightly forward and in a stage whisper called, "Foo-Foo Head."

The President immediately put on an expression of stark horror. A bouncing, gleeful little boy danced off to bed, confident that he had topped his dad at least on this day.

That bright, uninhibited boy saw in the world a series of new wonders endlessly appearing on the horizon. He hadn't seen my son, Paul, for more than a year, and during that time Paul had put about six inches on his fourteen-year-old frame.

When John saw Paul again, he recognized the face but was mystified by the body. Looking up at Paul for several seconds, he finally put the question directly to him: "Paul, are you a boy?"

On Good Friday afternoon of that Easter, 1963, weekend, Jack and I, accompanied by a strong contingent of "right-handers" from the Secret Service, drove to the Roman Catholic Church on Ocean Boulevard in Palm Beach to go to confession.

I think it is fair to say that most Catholics would rather go to confession to a priest they don't know, or one who at least doesn't know whose confession he is hearing. The President was no exception. As President of the United States, with his familiar voice and New England accent, he found it almost impossible to go to confession without being immediately recognized. If he happened to hit a gregarious confessor, the priest might find it difficult later to avoid speaking with a certain knowing authority about the President of the United States and his minor shortcomings. For this or other reasons the President tried to make arrangements so the priest never knew whose confession he had heard.

On one occasion, he had entered the confessional only to be greeted with the words, "Good evening, Mr. President."

"I replied, 'Good evening, Father,' and politely but quickly took my leave," Jack said with a touch of whimsey.

Now here in Palm Beach, he had the Secret Service men who were going to confession line up ahead of him. After the first of the agents had gone to confession, Jack slipped in ahead of the remaining three men. By changing his place in line, I'm sure he kept that a day of anonymous sinners.

In general, Jack felt about his religion as many Catholics

his age feel. Life was full and demanding and the need for religion generally seemed remote. But the basic faith acquired as a child in a Catholic family instilled in him a total allegiance to his faith that only real faith brings.

On the few occasions when we discussed our religion, he talked thoughtfully of the challenge facing the Church in the fast-changing world. With the universe opening up, science registering achievements never before conceived as within the grasp of man, the Church would surely have to change to meet the test of the times. His faith did not keep him from questioning his Church on positions that seemed in conflict with the needs of society.

After our confessions on that Good Friday, when we came out of the church, the priest, a monsignor the President had obviously known for some time, was out front to greet us. There were about twenty or so others also standing around chatting or just enjoying watching the President. A very gregarious individual, the monsignor took the President's arm and said, "Mr. President, I want you to meet some of my best parishioners." He then introduced him to a couple of wealthy-looking New York ladies in their early sixties, and one husband, all obviously down for the winter vacation period. After a brief exchange, the monsignor interrupted their conversation as though he had a very important, highly secret message to deliver to the President. Leading the President aside a few steps, he whispered something in his ear.

Jack pulled back with a look of mild humor on his face and said, "Father, if you have something like that to say, you don't have to whisper it."

When we got in the car, Jack said to me, "Do you know what that Father said when he drew me aside? He whispered in my ear, 'Mr. President, you're doing a wonderful job.' I told him, 'Father, you don't have to whisper that kind of news,' but that cagey old Irishman wasn't about to broadcast a statement like that in this Republican stronghold."

But going to church in Palm Beach lacked a very small but human incident that the President loved, which occurred every Sunday on the way to Mass in Hyannis. I first became conscious of it when I heard the President say to Bill Greer, his Secret Service driver, "Bill be sure we take the road we usually take to Mass. I don't want to miss my most ardent supporter."

Bill responded, "Absolutely, Mr. President. We'll go right by him."

Intrigued, I asked, "Who is this great fan?"

The President, with obvious pleasure, replied, "Down about six or eight blocks from the church there is an old-timer who stations himself out by his mailbox waiting for us to go by. He has to be in his eighties. He leans on a cane and when we come by, he gives the greatest toothless smile and eager wave you've ever seen."

Within about a half a block of his Sunday summer friend, Jack sat forward in his seat and told Bill Greer, "Slow down a little." Then, looking at me, he said, "There he is up there just around the corner."

As we made the turn, the old-timer broke into a tremendous smile, waving to the President as the President waved back at him. When we had passed, Jack turned to me. "If I had more supporters like that old pal it would be a joy to read the newspapers every day."

I question that there were many people who suffered a

greater personal loss than that old gentleman on the President's route to church.

One common way fathers have for demonstrating affection is throwing their children in the air. After the tree-planting episode in Canada, the President was denied this pleasure because of his bad back.

Instead, when the President arrived at Squaw Island for a weekend, he would fall to the grass in the area behind the house facing the sea, pulling John to him as he went down. John would try to get away, hoping to make his Dad chase him. During all the wrestling and tugging, the President would be saying something like, "John, aren't you lucky to have a Dad who plays with you like this?" or, "John, you don't seem to be acting as if you are enjoying being with your wonderful dad."

As I often tossed my children in the air when they were growing up, the President would ask me to toss John in the air also. When John saw me, he would run over, turn his back to me with his arms out and say, "Red, throw me up."

After witnessing one of these episodes, Pierre Salinger said, "Redhead, you might be loved around here now, but don't ever miss John, Jr. There will be a new Under Secretary of the Navy the next day."

I always was at my coordinated best.

During Teddy Kennedy's Senatorial campaign, the Bride and I were at the President's house in the compound at Hyannis Port one Saturday evening. This was in late August. The whole family had gathered there, and during the cocktail hour Teddy was planning to tell the others his ideas for his television debate with McCormack. It seemed that word had leaked out that McCormack was planning to cast his presentation chiefly as a personal attack on Teddy, rather than discussing the issues. Teddy was ready to meet fire with fire. "Eddie will get twice as much back as he gives out," he said.

The President was standing on his crutches, watching. After about ten minutes of the presentation, he broke in. "Now listen, Eddie," he said (he always called his youngest brother "Eddie"), "you forget any personal attack on Eddie McCormack. You're going to need all the supporters that McCormack has right after the primary. Let McCormack attack you as much as he wants. You're running for United States Senator. Stay on the issues and leave the personal attacks out."

Joseph Kennedy, still laboring under a speech handicap from his stroke, raised his finger in a counting motion, and forced out the words: "You do what Jack says."

Teddy acquiesced immediately and completely. Bob, Eunice, Sarge and Steve Smith indicated by their silence, nods or words that they fell right into line.

In a family of so many strong and positive personalities, it was also nice that the leader of the family happened to be the President of the United States.

CHAPTER TWENTY-THREE

NE SUNNY FRIDAY afternoon I was seated in the President's compartment of Air Force One. After gazing out thoughtfully at the blue sky and the scattered white clouds, the President turned to me and said, "Redhead, we travel pretty well." Then, as if he were looking in the future, he added: "But let's enjoy it. It's not going to last forever."

Although the President had his choice of the most luxurious homes in the United States, I always thought he relaxed most thoroughly when he was able to spend a weekend in a place he and Jacqueline rented at Squaw Island, on the Cape.

This rustic, weathered, comfortable, sprawling structure on

the edge of the Atlantic seemed to be everything Jack had ever wanted in a summer home. From the ocean side no other houses were visible—only the sea. Yet the Kennedy compound was almost within shouting distance.

Directly or indirectly, an approach had been made to the owners to see if they would sell, but no agreement had been reached. Evidently a price had been mentioned, because the President exclaimed, "That much for a house and one acre of land! People must still be reading that article in *Fortune*."

He was referring to an article that said that Joseph P. Kennedy was worth between two and four hundred million dollars.

I told the President that when it came to buying a house I didn't feel that the seller's price was the main consideration if you could afford to pay it.

"If I follow your philosophy, how is it going to look to a coal miner in West Virginia or an unemployed aircraft worker in your abundant state if the President of the United States is willing to cough up over $200,000 for a $150,000 house on one acre?" he asked. "Out near Atoka we could get a $75,000 house and probably over a couple of hundred acres of land for that price."

"Yes," I said, "but out there you end up with nothing but your couple of hundred acres. Here at your front door you have hundreds of thousands of acres of ocean which are all yours, and they don't cost you a cent."

He looked at me a moment and then said, "Grand Old Lovable, I never quite thought of it in that light. Maybe if we can't get this place, we can get that vacant land up near the water tank and build."

246

John Kennedy enjoyed the White House years. I remember one afternoon when I was sitting on the fantail of the *Honey Fitz* after a particularly good lunch. The President, who had gotten into the habit of smoking small cigars after the 1960 election, accepted one from the steward and then with a wide sweep of his arm pointed to me.

"Steward," he said, "give the Under Secretary of the Navy one of those fine White House cigars."

As though he were anticipating my possible refusal, he then turned to me and said, "Red, take one. There isn't a finer cigar being served in America today—at least not on the *Honey Fitz* today."

I accepted, of course, and we sat there in silence for a moment, looking out across the water and enjoying the Presidential cigars.

One of the most powerful and wealthiest men in the world, John Kennedy could get great pleasure from the simplest forms of relaxation—a movie, a game of golf, a swim, conversation with his friends or an afternoon automobile ride.

Shortly after he became President, Secret Serviceman Bill Greer drove us through the Virginia countryside on our way to Middleburg. Jack was always intensely interested in history, and he happened to notice an historical plaque beside the road.

"Bill," he called, "pull over to the marker."

Bill did, and I heard brakes screeching as half a dozen cars behind us pulled to a sudden stop.

We both turned around and looked back. The Secret Service cars that had been following us were turned this way and that all over the road to avoid hitting us. It was close. The President then said: "Can't you see the headlines: 'Secret Service Cars

Try to Get President in Auto Crash'?" Then he said, "Bill, we'll go through a little formation driving before we try that again."

One Thursday night the President rang me up at our home in McLean.

"Red we're going down to see the battlefield at Gettysburg on Saturday. Catch up on your Civil War history so I don't have to take you through grammar school history in front of your children. We're not going down just to stare blankly at rocks, fences and monuments."

Fortunately, we had two volumes on the Civil War published by American Heritage, which were excellent. My wife and I studied all Thursday evening and again on Saturday morning before starting on our caravan to the battlefields.

The President drove a Mercury with the top down. Jacqueline and Caroline were in the front seat, and Anita, Sally and I had the back seat. Our other two children, Kathy and Paul, were directly behind us in the first of four Secret Service cars.

Just before we reached the battlefield area, we picked up a history teacher from the local high school who doubled as a guide.

Rarely did a man have a more miserable time. The Fays, crammed with facts and figures, were ready to challenge him or demand clarification on every point. When I'd get too obnoxious, the President would interject: "Professor ————, don't hesitate to give us the facts. I happen to know the extent of Secretary Fay's Civil War knowledge."

As we traveled from battle area to battle area, I was fascinated by the reaction of other people visiting the battlefields.

248

As the First Family was dressed very informally, and the Mercury convertible was not what you would normally expect a President of the United States to come driving up in, most people didn't realize it was the President until they practically bumped into him. Most of them respected his privacy, but they would almost fall all over themselves trying to observe his every move.

The knowledge the President displayed about the Civil War amazed me. When we came to a certain area where a Boston or Massachusetts unit had fought, he recounted the battle with such detail that I could almost see it taking place. I kept expecting a Kelly or a Murphy to come charging up the gorge.

When we reached the place from which Pickett launched his charge, the battle was discussed at length. Before many minutes had passed, one of my previous idols, Robert E. Lee, was toppled from his pedestal. It seemed incomprehensible that he would have committed such a great force on a frontal attack uphill without waiting to learn whether Stuart's cavalry was ready to attack the Union forces from the rear. Stuart never appeared. Pickett's men were slaughtered.

"Mr. President, I'm surprised that Lee is held in such high esteem by the Southerners after such a catastrophe," I said.

"I'm sure there were some conditions behind his decisions that even the historians missed," the President said. "Besides, it had been a long campaign, and that may have sapped his strength. It's not fair to judge him a failure because of one defeat. Besides, he was more than just a military leader."

Golf had always been one of John Kennedy's favorite sports, and he played it well. But after he became President, the possibility of public criticism and the difficulty of enjoying a round quietly took some of the pleasure out of the game for him.

He was conscious of the exaggerated case Ike's detractors tried to build against him, charging him with neglect of duty because of his frequent escapes to the golf course.

John Kennedy felt strongly that the vitality of his administration could be weakened if it appeared that the Chief was neglecting his duties for long hours of recreation. The tabulation of Ike's hours on the golf course by some Washington reporters was still vividly remembered.

Knowing about this feeling, I was mildly surprised on a Friday afternoon in early February, 1961, by a phone call from Evelyn Lincoln. "Mr. Secretary," she said, "the President would like to have you come over tomorrow morning about twelve o'clock. Bring your golf clubs and clothes. He wants to play golf with you, George Smathers and Senator Symington."

I realized that day and on many other days how fortunate the President was to have Mrs. Lincoln for a secretary. She was an oasis of warmth and friendliness right outside his office door. Her office walls were lined with pictures of the President and his family and framed cartoons that tickled the President, and her desk always had vases of flowers and a box or bowl of candy. She liked and was liked by all the President's friends, but she also knew which ones he didn't want to be burdened with, and graciously shielded him from them. She knew instinctively when the President was disturbed and how much he needed a touch of levity or a relaxing moment with an old friend.

Often I would call Evelyn to leave a message for the President, not wanting to disturb him.

"Why don't you tell it directly to the President?" she would ask.

Then, while I was about to tell her that it wasn't that important, she would switch the phones and on would come that stimulating voice, saying something like: "Is it true that the admirals have you in the bag, and your old friend the President was just sold down the river to help the growing popularity of their ever-cooperative Under Secretary?"

If you happened to drop by to leave a message of no urgency for the President, you soon learned to preface your message with, "Now, Evelyn, I don't want to disturb the President, I just want to leave this message." Nine times out of ten, she would still take you on into his office or he would come out. Evelyn must have felt that those brief, nonbusiness visits with friends were a tonic to John Kennedy.

I often noticed the whimsical look on the President's face when he found three or four of his friends seemingly having a great time in Evelyn's office. As if he had been excluded from the pleasures, he'd say, "Well, at least one of us is trying to do a job for his country."

On this particular foggy Saturday morning I reached the President's office about 11:45. About 12:30, the President concluded his meetings and came into Evelyn's office exclaiming, "It's such a miserable day I told Smathers and Stu that golf would be impossible."

Then he continued, "Why don't we go out here in the Rose Garden and hit some? They say that Ike used to come out here and practice his irons. We'll get Muggsy O'Leary to shag for us."

Turning to Muggsy, who was carrying the bag of clubs and a ball bag as if they were suitcases, Jack started selling him

251

on the idea. Muggsy had the frank, unsophisticated look of a man who had never really asked too much of life and had gotten about what he expected—and a little more. Muggsy had met John Kennedy while serving on the Massachusetts Capitol Police Force, and on that day found his leader.

"Muggsy," the President said, "of all the people who would have cherished this opportunity, you have been selected to be the first person to shag for the thirty-fifth President of the United States."

"What is shag?" Muggsy asked, not especially impressed by this sudden honor.

In the fog that surrounded the White House that morning, even a skilled ball hawk would have had his problems tracking the golf balls. With Muggsy at the helm it looked to me as though the only possible result would be a lot of lost balls and Muggsy in the nearest hospital as a result of taking too many golf balls on the head and body.

"Muggsy, dump the balls here on the lawn," the President said. "Then take the bag and go out a ways, and we'll hit some iron shots at you." From the expression on Muggsy's face I wasn't convinced that Muggsy didn't see himself as the first true martyr of the New Frontier.

As we selected eight and nine irons to start with, Muggsy walked out about twenty yards and turned around, ready for us to start aiming at him.

The President said to me in a low voice, "Don't you get the impression that Muggsy hasn't quite grasped the true art of shagging?" Then to Muggsy: "Muggsy, you have to go out farther. Go across the road to the South Lawn."

Muggsy dutifully followed instructions and we started to

fire away. The balls would rise, disappear in the fog and then drop somewhere in the vicinity of Muggsy.

Deciding after a few minutes that Muggsy was sure to get hit, the President called out: "Muggsy, you're too valuable to this administration to risk you out there. Go back under cover. We'll have someone go out when the fog clears and pick up the balls." With Muggsy out of danger, we began hitting the balls in earnest.

No one was more flattering to play or practice golf with than John Kennedy. He treated me as though I'd just come off the winter circuit and asked questions that seemed to indicate that my counsel was the last word.

"What am I doing wrong?" he would ask. "Almost every shot I hit is a hook."

I'd come back with advice that any weekend golfer under a twelve handicap could give: "Slow down your back swing and make it a little more upright."

If he hit the next couple of shots relatively straight, he would say, "Redhead, you've cured me. You diagnosed me perfectly." When he hit a real blast, he'd say, "Arnie would have been proud of that shot."

I often wondered whether Arnold Palmer knew how much the President admired him. I met Palmer only once, briefly, with Billy Breslan, in the steam room at the Olympic Club in San Francisco, but from that one meeting and from what I have heard about him it is too bad that he and John Kennedy didn't know each other. They would have been good friends.

Still hitting balls, after working up from the eight and nine to the three and four, Jack started to hit with his three wood. The balls were sailing into the trees down toward the east gate.

Suddenly he asked me, "If you hit a driver or brassie with everything you have, right on the screws, do you think you could hit one out of the grounds?"

"There's only one way to find out," I said. And then I added: "Can't you see the expression on the face of some farmer in from Dubuque, Iowa, with his wife, strolling around their White House for the first time when suddenly a golf ball drops out of the fog and bounces down the street?"

With that I started to swing away in earnest. The balls flew out over the Rose Garden, across the South Lawn, up over the trees. Because of the fog, it was hard to tell if I ever made it. The only way I'll ever find out is if someone reads this who remembers a golf ball bouncing by them on a February afternoon in 1961 on the east side of the White House and lets me know.

Occasionally the President combined his profession of politics with his relaxation at golf. One Saturday in early 1961 I drove out to the Chevy Chase Club with him to play golf with Senator Stuart Symington and Senator George Smathers.

On the way to the club, I asked him what he thought of the idea of Barney Ross coming to Washington to help in the government's program on juvenile delinquency.

"His way with young people is unbelievable," I said. "They not only love to be with him; they trust him and have confidence in him."

"What is he doing now?" the President asked. "Has he had any experience or training in juvenile education or training?"

"No, he hasn't any formal training in the juvenile delinquent area," I said. "Presently he is working as an insurance salesman. But few people instill trust or confidence as quickly as

Barney. All the formal education available can't provide the sincerity and dedication that Barney could give to the unprivileged."

"All right," he said with a trace of impatience, "so you want Barney in Washington. How much should he be paid? What's he getting now?"

"He is making about $7,500 a year, but he'd have to have at least $12,500 to cover his additional expenses coming to Washington. Of course, Barney in his usual self-effacing man ner says he isn't worth $12,500 and doesn't want to come down here and embarrass you and have people saying, 'The President is finding a spot for an old shipmate to give him a helping hand.' Besides the job will only last eight years."

The President caught the two-term inference and interjected flatly, "Let's get Barney settled here before we start making plans so he can grow old gracefully. If he is worried about the $12,500, have him work harder."

"Well, that's it," I said. "All I need is the okay from you that you would like him in the delinquent program, and I'll work it out with Bob and Dave Hackett."

"All right," he said. "He should do a good job. Go ahead."

Barney did a good job. In fact, he worked his head off, bringing credit and pride to the President.

But then, having given his approval, he mused aloud: "I wonder if this administration is strong enough to survive George Ross, Red Fay, 'McNamara's Band' and 'Hooray for Hollywood.'"

As soon as we reached the club, we drove to a tee far out on the course to avoid any photographers who might have been tipped off that the President was going to play golf.

255

"If the word leaks out," Jack said, "I can just see some eager reporter writing, 'The new President couldn't even wait until the snow was off the ground before engaging in his first game of golf as President. At this rate President Kennedy could devote more time to the golf links than his predecessor.' "

I was intrigued during Ike's Presidency by newspaper photographs of Secret Service men walking along on the edge of the fairways carrying golf bags, with the butts of rifles or machine guns sticking from the top. That day at the Chevy Chase Club, I saw the same Secret Service men trying to look like golfers—bad ones, because they spent all their time in the rough. They were as conspicuous out on the course as someone attending a formal dinner in a sport shirt.

The President indicated that he and I were to be partners playing against George and Stuart.

"Smathers, it is common knowledge that you are probably the finest golfer on the Hill, which in no way implies the slightest dereliction of duty," the President said. "Stu is one of those few naturally gifted golfers, but in spite of the obvious overwhelming odds, Red and I will still take you on."

He hadn't allowed for an answer, so none was forthcoming.

Because of the snow, we weren't permitted to go onto the greens. Large six-inch diameter cans had been embedded in the turf in front of the regular greens and the grass had been clipped as short as possible so these areas could serve as temporary greens.

To keep some distance from the clubhouse, we made up our holes as we went along, sometimes hitting from one tee across several fairways to the "hole" of another fairway.

At one juncture we passed Phyllis Dillon, wife of the new

256

Secretary of the Treasury. She and her companion played rather nervously under the appraising eye of the young President. Phyllis said later, "If I could have picked up my ball and run, I would have been a lot happier. I'm just not accustomed to holding up the play of the President of the United States."

During one stage of the game the President wanted to get in touch with Stewart Udall for some reason. The Secret Service man with the walkie-talkie was flagged and came over immediately to transmit the President's message, but the Secretary of Interior could not be located.

In a flash of humor, the young President asked, "How are we supposed to run a government if the people in positions of responsibility aren't available when needed?"

On the seventh green, photographers and newspapermen were waiting. The President had some governmental matter on his mind, and that, along with the sight of the newspapermen, was enough to end the game. The Presidential limousine was called, and soon appeared on the course. Almost before those waiting for him were conscious of it, he was in his limousine and gone.

Just as suddenly, the bond was broken between the two Senators and myself. We didn't even bother to play out the hole, but instead went our separate ways. The excitement of our game had also disappeared in that limousine.

CHAPTER TWENTY-FOUR

N THE SPRING of 1963 one of the news agencies carried a story speculating over whether the President would stick with Lyndon Johnson in 1964 or dump him for another Vice Presidential candidate. That article marked the beginning of a wave of speculation over the relationship between the President and the Vice President. There were rumors in Washington that John Kennedy himself had planted the first report about Johnson being dropped to prepare the way for his search for a new running mate.

This talk surprised me, because the President often complimented Johnson publicly and privately, and had always been

258

unusually solicitous of the Vice President. One Saturday morning in the Oval Office I asked the President, "Is there any truth to the rumor that you intend to dump Lyndon in '64?"

I don't know whether it was the word "dump" that irritated him or the entire subject, but that handsome face suddenly flushed with anger.

"What do you mean, am I going to dump Johnson in '64? What do you ask a question like that for? Of course I'm not. He's doing an excellent job in the most thankless position in Washington. He's my man for the job. He's going to be my man in '64, and I don't know why you're asking. I don't think the question was necessary."

He was beginning to think more and more about the 1964 campaign, and one Saturday morning in the spring of 1963 he said to me, "The one fellow I don't want to run against is Romney. That guy could be tough. But give me good old Barry. I'd never have to leave this Oval Office."

He added: "You have to be a little suspicious of somebody as good as Romney. No vices whatsoever, no smoking and no drinking. Imagine someone we know going off for twenty-four or forty-eight hours to fast and meditate, awaiting a message from the Lord whether to run or not to run. Does that sound like one of the old gang?"

Then, as if he were not sure whether he had revealed too much of his thoughts, he looked squarely at me and said, "That's a bit of information that is not to go any farther than this office. Let the Republicans choose their own candidate free of outside influences."

I asked him about the more remote future one day while we were strolling toward the next tee at the Hyannis Golf Course.

"What are you going to do after you've had eight years in the White House?"

He looked at me first as though he were reflecting about whether I should have asked the question. Then, with a tone of authority, he replied, "We've got four we're working on right now. We'll worry about the next four when the time comes."

Feeling there was still an open end, I persisted, "All right, say everything falls into place. You have eight years as President behind you, what then?"

As if he were savoring the thought of being an elder statesman while still young, with the prestige of his Presidential years but without the demanding day-by-day responsibility, he said, "We could go back to the South Pacific and revisit those waters where we personally almost turned the tide of war. Then drift through the Greek islands. . . ."

Then, he answered seriously, "I'd run for the Senate."

"But isn't it quite a comedown from being the President of the United States?" I asked.

Unimpressed by my question, he reminded me, "John Quincy Adams served in the House after being President. If a man came from the White House to the Congress, he could give a voice of judgment and authority to the legislative branch that would elevate the whole body. No, I think being a Senator after being a President is a good job and important."

Epilogue

Often now I find myself remembering one evening up at the Cape in November, 1961. The President had been working with great concentration on his budget on the Friday and

260

Saturday after Thanksgiving, but he joined the other members of the family, my wife and myself up at his father's house for cocktails and dinner on Saturday night.

He was pleased by the accomplishments of that week, and after dinner he suggested that I sing "Hooray for Hollywood." I said I would if everyone else would agree to perform.

I blasted out my specialty, Teddy sang "Heart of My Heart," and Eunice also sang, while Joan played the piano. Then everyone in the room insisted that the President sing.

"Do you know the 'September Song'?" he asked Joan. She played the chorus two or three times, and then the President began to sing those haunting words:

> Oh, it's a long, long while
> From May to December,
> But the days grow short
> When you reach September. . . .

The earlier performances had been greeted with boisterous, friendly clapping, but now we were all silent. Suddenly I realized as I never had before that these days were rushing past, that we were living in a time that could never be regained. Then he spoke the next lines:

> Oh, the days dwindle down
> To a precious few,
> September, November!
> And these few precious days
> I'll spend with you. . . .*

We did not know then that the extraordinary man who had already achieved so much would not live to see the September

* Copyright © 1938 by DeSylva, Brown & Henderson, Inc. Copyright renewed. Used by permission.

of his own life, but would die in the blazing summer of his youth.

Each year, as the month of November approaches, I, like hundreds of millions of other people all over the world, cannot escape the recollection of those senseless shots on a Dallas street. But we must never let John Kennedy's tragic death obscure or shadow the triumphant victory of his life.